Studies on Chronic Mental Illness: New Horizons for Social Work Researchers

Joan P. Bowker and Allen Rubin, Editors

Council on Social Work Education

11-16-87

Copyright © 1986 by the Council on Social Work Education, Inc.

The opinions expressed in this publication are solely those of the contributors and do not necessarily reflect the policy or position of the Council on Social Work Education. No official endorsement of the views presented should be inferred unless it is so indicated.

Library of Congress Catalog Card Number: 87-70074
ISBN: 0-87293-015-7

Council on Social Work Education
1744 R Street, N.W.
Washington, D.C. 20009
(202) 667-2300

Printed in the United States of America.

Table of Contents

PART II: RESEARCH DESIGN

PART III: CONCLUSION

Acknowledgments

The papers in this book were originally presented at a conference entitled "The Chronically Mentally Ill: Improving the Knowledge Base through Research," sponsored by the Council on Social Work Education in Washington, D.C., June 13-14, 1985. The conference brought together experienced and beginning researchers from social work and the social sciences to present their current research on services to the chronically mentally ill, to learn from each other, and to kindle their excitement anew.

All of the participants in the conference—sponsors, presenters, and audience—contributed to the excitement, and the editors gratefully acknowledge them. The names with asterisks were conference program presenters or moderators.

*Leona Bachrach
 Maryland Psychiatric Research Center

 Rosalyn Bass
 National Institute of Mental Health

*L. Diane Bernard
 Council on Social Work Education

*Joseph Bevilacqua
 Virginia Department of Mental Health

 Richard Blake
 Rutgers University, Newark

 Joan P. Bowker
 Council on Social Work Education

 Kaaren Brown
 Eastern Michigan University

 Neal Brown
 National Institute of Mental Health

Beulah Compton
The University of Alabama

*Kenneth Cooley
Veterans Administration

*Claudia Coulton
Case Western Reserve University

King Davis
Virginia Department of Mental Health

*Laura Davis
University of Wyoming

*Ann Denton
University of Texas, Austin

*Susan Eddy
State University of New York, Stony Brook

Phillip Fellin
The University of Michigan

Joel Fischer
University of Hawaii

Paul Freddolino
Michigan State University

*Howard Goldman
National Institute of Mental Health

*Courtenay Harding
Yale University

*Mary Harper
National Institute of Mental Health

Agnes Hatfield
University of Maryland

*Srinika Jayaratne
The University of Michigan

Wyatt Jones
Brandeis University

Maryanne Keenan
Council on Social Work Education

*Stuart Kirk
State University of New York, Albany

Jean Marie Kruzich
University of Wisconsin, Milwaukee

Alice Lieberman
University of Southern Maine

Edie Maeda
Woodley House, Washington

*Ronald Manderscheid
National Institute of Mental Health

*Lynn McDonald-Wikler
Univeristy of Wisconsin, Madison

Matthew Modrcin
University of Kansas

Donald Moses
Veterans Administration

Donald Mowry
University of Wisconsin, Madison

*David Moxley
Wayne State University

Edward Mullen
University of Chicago

Elane Neuhring
Barry University

Carolyn Peabody
State University of New York

Dorothy Pearson
Howard University

*Juan Ramos
National Institute of Mental Health

*Charles Rapp
University of Kansas

Cheryl Richey
University of Washington

Daniel Rodel
Veterans Administration

Jacqueline Rosenberg
National Institute of Mental Health

*Allen Rubin
University of Texas, Austin

Connie Saltz
Veterans Administration

David Saunders
Virginia Commonwealth University

Leslie Scallett
Policy Resources, Inc.

James Schmidt
Fountain House

*Steven P. Segal
University of California, Berkeley

*Barbara Shore
University of Pittsburgh

*Carol G. Simonetti
The Cleveland Foundation

*Phyllis Solomon
Cleveland Federation for Community Planning

*LeRoy Spaniol
Boston University Center for Research and Training in
    Mental Health

Samuel Taylor
University of Southern California

Robert Teare
University of Alabama

Anthony Zipple
Boston University Center for Research and Training in
    Mental Health

Special thanks are due the Council on Social Work Education and to L. Diane Bernard, its Interim Executive Director.

The editors wish to express their profound gratitude to Peter Whitten for his editorial work.

The conference was supported by grant #MH17923 from the National Institute of Mental Health, Social Work Education Program, to the CSWE Curriculum and Resource Development Project on Chronic Mental Illness.

Joan P. Bowker
Project Director
Council on Social Work Education
Curriculum and Resource
    Development Project on
    Chronic Mental Illness

Allen Rubin
Associate Professor
School of Social Work
University of Texas
    at Austin

Preface

L. Diane Bernard

As Interim Executive Director of the Council on Social Work Education, it was my pleasure, in June 1985, to welcome to Washington a group of experts deeply committed to posing questions about services to the chronically mentally ill person and finding, through their research, the answers to those questions. Many critical questions relating to improvement of the quality of life of sadly neglected people were addressed. I was struck, for example, by Leona Bachrach's reminder of the importance, in the conduct of research on mental patients, of raising the right questions with a sensitivity to cultural relevance. And Stuart Kirk, in his excellent summary, provides insight into the process by which social injustice becomes defined as a social problem and is legitimized as an appropriate subject for research and public policy initiatives. This collection of papers identifies the myriad of social problems experienced by the chronically mentally ill. In our response to this special population, it is important that we, as social workers, remain sensitive to injustice and continue to raise the right research questions.

On a personal note, I am interested to see the new attention given to the needs of families who care for their chronically mentally ill relative. I would like to see this work extended to examine the cost of mental illness to the women in our society who have borne the brunt of the deinstitutionalization movement. The current emphasis in service strategies and federal research priorities is on maximizing the contribution of families in the care of the chronically mentally ill. Such a focus should not go unexamined, as it is tantamount to a public policy that encourages women to give priority to responsibilities in the home, since the unpaid service provider is invariably the nearest female relative, whose care-giving work goes unrecognized as "real work" and is therefore unregulated by law or unions. Women are involved in ever-increasing numbers in the work force, with no recognition or respite provided from care-giving duties. The costs borne by women include lost income, isolation, depression, decline in health, loss of pensions, and security. While care giving in behalf of society is no new role for women, the burden has actually expanded with the aging of the population, deinstitutionalization, and reduced public funds for all dependent groups. As we reassess deinstitutionalization and understand the unanticipated consequences that have spawned new problems, we must also study the injustice and societal costs that women bear as primary caretakers.

I found these papers to be highly provocative. I thank all of those who attended the conference for their considerable contributions. They raise new issues that precede the next round of research questions addressing the problems of the chronically mentally ill.

Introduction

Historical Underpinnings and Current Issues for Social Work Research on Chronic Mental Illness

Allen Rubin

Recent mental health policy has shifted the prime location of care for persons suffering from chronic mental illness from institutions to communities, in what has been termed the deinstitutionalization movement. Despite the noble goals of that movement, we now know that rather than substantially improving the plight of the chronically mentally ill, it has merely continued the long history of neglect of this population, a neglect that has been sustained throughout several eras of reform that managed to change the location of care but failed to garner adequate public fiscal support for that care (Morrissey & Goldman, 1984). Today, as we hear about the large numbers of persons with chronic mental illness who are homeless or who are being dealt with as criminal offenders, we are reminded of prior centuries, when such people were cast out of town as "wandering fools" or lumped with criminals and paupers in workhouses (Grob, 1973).

To some, deinstitutionalization has meant a freeing of victims from inhumane state hospitals where they were held in violation of their civil liberties. Others, however, recall that state hospitals were created after a crusade by Dorothea Dix over a century ago to provide asylum and sanctuary to individuals too sick to fend for themselves in communities that did not want them and stigmatized them. Dorothea Dix's movement succeeded in getting public mental hospitals built, but securing enough fiscal support to ensure humane conditions in them was another matter. State hospitals were built with minimal expenditures and inferior construction; without adequate resources, Dix's reform soon produced unintended consequences—overcrowded, inhumane warehouses where chronically mentally ill persons unable to afford expensive private care could be dumped, neglected, and forgotten (Grob, 1973).

Deinstitutionalization is not a new idea. During the first decade of the twentieth century, a movement emerged to return patients from mental hospitals to communities, a movement whose aims and means foreshadowed many current concepts of community-based care (Lubove, 1977; Mechanic, 1969). Such aftercare was one of the central tenets of psychiatric social work at its inception as a profession (Lubove, 1979). This focus, however, was short-lived. As epidemic diseases were being conquered, the mental hygiene and child guidance movements popularized the belief that, like contagious diseases, mental illness could be prevented, particularly by intervening during childhood. Overly zealous belief in psychoanalytic theory further fostered the notion that early psychodynamic interventions offered a panacea for dealing with mental illness, making environmentally-oriented aftercare with already chronic cases seem less attractive as either a form of practice or as a strategy in which to invest (Morrissey & Goldman, 1984; Lubove, 1977). Why expend scarce resources on caring for debilitated casualties who have limited potential when other approaches promise to prevent mental illness or cure it before it becomes chronic? Several decades were thus typified by continued neglect of persons suffering from chronic mental illness, as they received care in most state hospitals, and psychiatric social workers and other mental health professionals pursued what seemed to be more promising agendas (Morrissey & Goldman, 1979; Hogarty, 1971).

In 1955, psychotropic drugs were discovered, allowing better control of the symptomatology of mental illness and increasing the rate of discharges from state hospitals. Thus began the deinstitutionalization movement. During the 1960s and early 1970s, deinstitutionalization was spurred by several developments: (1) advances in psychopharmacology; (2) litigation protecting patients' civil liberties with respect to commitment and institutionalization; (3) growth of community mental health centers (CMHCs) and other human-service programs, and attendant beliefs that these community-based facilities would care for chronically mentally ill individuals and thus offset the need for institutionalization; (4) fiscal crises in state governments in the early 1970s that led states to pass the problem to the federal level, with the rationale that Medicaid-Medicare funds and CMHCs would permit massive discharges from state hospitals; and (5) the growing belief that community-based care was cheaper, less restrictive, and more humane than institutional care (Morrissey & Goldman, 1984).

The 1970s, however, produced growing evidence that chronically mentally ill individuals do not always fare well in the community. They often live in squalor and are rejected, even victimized, by their neighbors. Conditions of community-based care were deemed by some to be as bad as the back wards of state hospitals and by others to be the same conditions that led to the nineteenth century reforms that created state hospitals (Morrissey & Goldman, 1984). In most localities, service delivery systems were not sufficient to meet the full range of needs of the chronically mentally ill—the for drug maintenance and monitoring, vocational rehabilitation, transitional or other living arrangements, social and recreational activities, resocialization in basic living skills, supportive counseling, financial assistance, assistance in household management, health care, and family intervention for individuals residing with their families. Community agencies that theoretically could address the above needs were often unresponsive to prospective clients suffering from chronic mental illness. Even community mental health centers responded inadequately, due to funding inducements and staff preferences that favored work with insured, nonchronic clientele (General Accounting Office, 1978). As the professional literature and mass media began to expose these problems, we learned that the mere presence of expanded services in the community did not mean that chronically mentally ill individuals would receive those services. We also learned that community settings are not necessarily less restrictive or more humane than the protected institutional environment (Bachrach, 1980). Indeed, the term *transinstitutionalization* has been proposed to depict more accurately the process of deinstitutionalization that was actually carried out (Morrissey & Goldman, 1984). That is, rather than being deinstitutionalized, the chronically mentally ill were moved from one restrictive setting to another, to living under conditions of institutionalization in community settings rather than in state hospitals.

During the late 1970s the National Institute of Mental Health (NIMH) responded to criticisms of community-based treatment failure by funding demonstration projects in 19 states to implement and test a strategy to integrate services in comprehensive community support systems. The community support program recognized the need to induce community-based agencies, including community mental health programs, to serve people suffering from chronic mental illness. This strategy allocated special coordinating power and authority to a specified local agency that would assess the needs of chronically mentally ill persons in its area, negotiate interagency linkage and agreements for providing all needed support services, and develop new service components to correct gaps in the service network (Turner, 1977; Turner & Shiffren, 1979; Turner & TenHoor, 1978).

In 1978 the President's Commission on Mental Health, deeming chronic mental illness to be a national priority, called for a better partnership between federal and state mental health programs. The commission noted the tendency of federally funded mental health programs to bypass states and the related tendency by community mental health center staff to assign extremely low priority to the objective of integration with state hospitals. These tendencies occurred despite the fact that the original intent of the "bold new approach" of community mental health legislation was, in large part, to offset long-term institutionalization in state hospitals (President's Commission on Mental Health, 1978).

The Mental Health Systems Act, enacted in 1980, sought to operationalize some of the commission's recommendations for increasing the role of the states in planning and administering mental health services—and thus to effect greater coordination between federal (community mental health) and state (state hospital) services. The legislation also sought to provide federal funding to enable states and local agencies to establish community support systems. Following the 1980 national election, however, the major provisions of the act were repealed. In 1981 the authorization of federal funds to establish community-based services was eliminated. Part of the intent of the act—to better integrate state and federal services for the chronically mentally ill—was achieved by consolidating all federal funds for alcohol, drug abuse, and mental health programs into a block grant to the states, with increased state authority over expenditures. But this was done with a reduced level of funding'' (Morrissey & Goldman, 1984).

Concern about the foregoing problems of deinstitutionalization and doubt about the likelihood of adequate financing of community support systems has led to widespread skepticism about the prospects for ''creating and sustaining a truly humane system of care for the dependent mentally ill'' (Morrissey & Goldman, 1984). Some advocates of humane care are even rediscovering the positive functions of institutions, such as the asylum and sanctuary for the most chronic and disabled of the mentally ill (Lamb & Peele, 1984). Likewise, the field is beginning to understand the diversity in the nature and degree of impairment among persons termed chronically mentally ill, and is realizing that some people are better off in one locus of care, while others are better off in another. It is the fit between person and environment that matters most (Coulton et al., 1985).

For some, the real issue is not so much the locus of care as our society's willingness to allocate sufficient resources to care fully for persons with chronic mental illness—whether in properly staffed and equipped state hospitals (for those who need that environment) or by comprehensive, adequately funded and staffed community support systems (Morrissey & Goldman, 1984). As this book goes to press, the care of persons suffering from chronic mental illness once again is being given lip service in federal mental health policy. Yet, as has happened before, that policy is being implemented with funds that may be insufficient to provide an adequate system of care for persons who, to paraphrase Leona Bachrach (1980), have severe and unremitting psychopathology and who reside primarily in communities that do not want them and often victimize them, communities where they will need long-term care from psychiatric and other support services for perhaps the rest of their lives.

As a policy, the recent deinstitutionalization experience parallels the history of the state hospital reform of the 19th century. Both eras sought to make the care and living conditions of persons with chronic mental illness more humane, and both sought to do this by shifting the locus of care. But neither was able to secure sufficient public fiscal support to create the humane environment that was envisioned. Several papers in this book review studies that empirically support the efficacy of some well-funded community-based programs. It is important to bear in mind that the findings of those studies do *not* mean that such programs work better than *adequately funded* institutionally-based programs or that other community-based programs— with less funding—are similarly effective. That is, despite the importance of developing new models of service delivery, it is not enough merely to test the efficacy of those models under ideal, well-endowed circumstances as compared to control conditions. We must ask: What makes these models work better? Is it their technology? Or is it their resources? How would their outcomes compare to those of preexisting technologies that are delivered with greater funding and a more enthused staff? And would the positive outcomes of the new models be upheld if implemented under less ideal circumstances? For example, if one study finds case managers with caseloads of 30 patients to be effective, is it reasonable to expect comparable outcomes from other case managers, working in another region and with less funds, with caseloads of 250 patients?

SOCIAL WORK'S CONTRIBUTION

Despite the preference by many social workers not to work with persons suffering from chronic mental illness, the profession has been instrumental in advancing concern and knowledge about this population. An analysis of recent social work research in mental health found more published articles on chronic mental illness than on any other mental health topic. This literature has generated useful knowledge about the needs and problems of persons with chronic mental illness and how the profession can serve them effectively. It also has reflected the significant progress being made by the profession's research enterprise (Rubin & Gibelman, 1984).

In light of this progress, the Council on Social Work Education's Curriculum and Resource Development Project on Chronic Mental Illness convened an invited forum entitled "Chronic Mental Illness: Improving the Knowledge Base Through Research." The forum, held in Washington, D.C. on June 13-14, 1985, brought together a small group of expert researchers with proven records of methodologically sophisticated published research studies in the field of chronic mental illness. The forum sought to identify major issues in contemporary practice and in education for practice with the chronic population, to define major research questions in the field, and to illustrate how innovative methodologies can be applied to those questions. The ultimate goal of the forum was to stimulate new research building upon the cumulative work already done.

PURPOSE AND PLAN OF THE BOOK

This book consists of some of the papers that were presented at the CSWE forum. The papers underwent editorial refinements subsequent to the meeting. Like the forum, the aim of this book is to stimulate additional research by social workers in the field of chronic mental illness—research that will build upon the findings that previous studies have accumulated. This book also seeks to stir enthusiasm about working in the field of chronic mental illness—either from a research or practice perspective—among faculty and students who have not been previously active in it. When teachers and students learn how effective interventions in this field can be, and as they see the rich research possibilities in it, they will become more likely to research it, to practice in it, and to teach about it. But the issue is not to promote one field of social work as more important than another. The point is that the work that has been completed in this field offers remarkable opportunities for social work researchers or practitioners who seek effective forms of practice or a body of research that they can be inspired by, learn from, and build upon.

This volume has three sections. Part I reviews the research literature, identifies unresolved issues, and develops implications for the formulation of additional research. This section is useful for those seeking empirical findings to guide their practice (or to teach about it). It also will be useful to individuals seeking guidance in the formulation of research problems that are based on current theory and research and which are likely to have practical importance. Doctoral students, for example, are likely to find a wealth of interesting dissertation ideas in this section.

Part II is more useful for researchers than to those seeking practice information. This section deals with some of the promising methodologies that social work researchers have been applying to the research questions identified in the first section. The point of Part II is not to provide textbook-like coverage of all research designs but to give readers an opportunity to learn from the experiences of noted social work researchers about the advantages, disadvantages, and unresolved issues in the methodologies for which these researchers are known. Included in this material is discussion of the feasibility of these methodologies. Feasibility is an important topic for social work researchers: novice researchers quickly learn that designing an ideal study is relatively easy; the hard part is finding ways to carry out the study without sacrificing too much methodological credibility.

The final section of the volume summarizes the material in Parts I and II and adds perspective on that material.

Social work researchers are building knowledge cumulatively on chronic mental illness, and are doing so with methodological sophistication. The papers in this book produce insights about promising new methodologies—in longitudinal research, single-subject designs, or assessments of person-environment fit—that are well-suited for addressing research questions still unanswered. One such question would ask: What works? In an institutional context, what outcomes might be achieved if the resources allocated to community-based facilities were allocated to upgrading institutional care? "Outcome" here does not necessarily have to do with cure of psychopathology; it might have more to do with the quality of a person's living conditions and social functioning while undergoing social care in a protected environment. Or one might assess what happens to chronic patients when a community-based program with inadequate funds attempts to implement components of a model program that was successful, with much greater fiscal support, elsewhere. For example, the Texas Department of Mental Health and Mental Retardation currently is relying on a community-based case management strategy in response to court-ordered reductions in state hospital patient-staff ratios. Yet their community-based staff complain that because this is done with inadequate state fiscal support, case managers' caseload sizes are near 250.

Another line of research would attempt to sort out the differential effectiveness of the components of various packages of interventions for families with persons who suffer from schizophrenia. Also needed are replications of outcome studies—replications that pay more heed to ensuring that outcome measures are not influenced by potential rater or staff biases. The type of residential environment that is most appropriate for a specific type of chronic patient is another critical question, one that can be addressed utilizing Claudia Coulton's material in chapter 7 on assessing person-environment fit. More research is also needed on the specific methods of intervention that produce specific outcomes with specific types of chronic patients. Chapter 6, by Sriniki Jayaratne, addresses the application of single-subject designs to this question.

These are just a few of the many promising lines of research that can be pursued in the near future. The social work profession has shown that it is capable of tackling these questions with methodological sophistication, and this book attempts to stimulate even greater advances in this endeavor.

REFERENCES

Bachrach, L. (1984). The concept of young adult chronic psychiatric patients: Questions from a research perspective. *Hospital and Community Psychiatry, 35*(6), 573-580.

Bachrach, L. (1983). Concepts and issues in deinstitutionalization. In I. Barofsly & R.D. Budson (Eds.), *The chronic psychiatric patients in the community.* New York: SP Medical & Scientific Books.

Bachrach, L. (1982). Young adult chronic patients. An analytical review of the literature. *Hospital and Community Psychiatry, 33*(3), 189-197.

Bachrach, L. (1980). Is the least restrictive environment always the best? Sociological and semantic implications. *Hospital and Community Psychiatry, 31*(2), 97-103.

Coulton, D., Fitch, F., & Holland, T. (1985). A typology of social environments in community care homes. *Hospital and Community Psychiatry, 35*(4), 373-377.

General Accounting Office (1978). *Returning the mentally disabled to the community: Government needs to do more.* Washington, D.C.: General Accounting Office.

Grob, G. (1973). *Mental institutions in America.* New York: The Free Press.

Hogarty, G. (1971). The plight of schizophrenics in modern treatment programs. *Hospital and Community Psychiatry, 1,* 197-203.

Lamb, H. Richard & Peele, R. (1984). The need for continuing asylum and sanctuary. *Hospital and Community Psychiatry, 35*(8), 798-802.

Lubove, R. (1977). *The professional altruist.* New York: Antheneum.

Mechanic, D. (1969). *Mental health and social policy.* Englewood Cliffs, New Jersey: Prentice-Hall.

Morissey, J. & Goldman, H. (1984). Cycles of reform in the care of the chronically mentally ill. *Hospital and Community Psychiatry, 35*(8), 785-793.

President's Commission on Mental Health (1978). *Report to the president: Mental health in America,* Vol. II. Washington, D.C.: U.S. Government Printing Office.

Rubin, A. (1984). Community-based care of the mentally ill: A research review. *Health and Social Work, 9,* 165-177.

Rubin, A. & Gibelman, M. (1984). *Social work research in mental health: The state of the art.* National Institute of Mental Health.

Rubin, A. & Johnson, P. (1982). Practitioner orientations toward serving the chronically mentally disabled: Prospects for policy implementation. *Administration In Mental Health, 10*(1), 3-12.

Turner, J. & Shiffren, I. (1979). Community support system: How comprehensive? In Stein, L. (Ed.), *Community support systems for the long-term patient.* San Francisco, CA: Jossey-Bass, Inc.

Turner, J. & TenHoor, W. (1978). The NIMH community support program: Pilot approach to a needed social reform. *Schizophrenia Bulletin, 4*(3), 319-349.

Turner, J. (1977). Comprehensive community support systems for severely disabled adults. *Psychosocial Rehabilitation Journal, 1*(1), 39-47.

PART I: PROBLEM FORMULATION

Introduction

Allen Rubin

The earliest stages in the research process, when problems are selected and formulated, have a critical influence upon the success and ultimate value of a research study. If inadequate attention is paid to the beginning stages, a researcher will waste resources later pursuing answers to questions that are infeasible to answer, that no one cares about, or that have been posed in the wrong way. One of the important early activities of the research process is the literature review. A common mistake made by novice researchers—doctoral students contemplating their dissertations, for example—is to put off their literature review until they have framed a narrow research question and formulated a preliminary design to investigate it. They may feel it is inefficient to review the literature before they have established their particular area of focus. The problem with that notion is that until they review the literature, they have no way of knowing which research questions have already been answered (perhaps including the ones they had in mind), the conceptual and practical obstacles already encountered in some lines of research, how others have overcome those obstacles, and what lines of research can build upon previous research.

Part I of this volume, which reviews the social work-related research literature on chronic mental illness, illustrates the value of conducting a thorough literature review early in one's research. Readers contemplating chronic mental illness as a field for their own research will find a number of important lines of research in this material—research that will have practical value in building upon current theory and empirical findings and in answering the most critical questions facing the field. This material might also stimulate interest in this field among some researchers whose interests previously lay elsewhere. And it may be of value to practitioners seeking more empirical support for practice efficacy or to educators seeking information about methods or fields of practice that can be better integrated with valid research.

A recurrent theme in Part I is the substantiation of supportive, educational approaches to assisting families living with a person who is chronically mentally ill. When using this research as an exemplar in my second-year master's-level research course, I have been struck by the dogmatism with which direct-practice students cling to family systems therapy despite their inability, in semester-long projects, to identify valid experimental research that supports the efficacy of their practice. I have been further impressed at their lack of familiarity with research showing that their form of practice is likely to be harmful when applied to families with chronically mentally ill members. Clearly, direct-practice instructors should be covering the implications of this theory and research in their teaching.

Family interventions are only one area in which social work educators may benefit from the material in Part I. Other areas will be evident, such as case management, social skills training, and practitioner attitudes about chronicity and social care as contrasted with curative and psychotherapeutic forms of practice with less disabled populations.

An overview of the research in this field is provided in chapter 1—an overview that focuses primarily on three types of research: (1) experimental outcome studies of effective forms of community-based care; (2) service-delivery studies documenting gaps between the type of care experimentally supported in model programs and the inadequacies of more typical programs of care; and (3) studies of attributes of residential environments and the attributes of those chronically impaired individuals best and least suited for different residential environments.

In chapter 2, Leona Bachrach presents a critique of the conceptual issues that plague research in this field, most notably regarding the concepts of "community support systems," "young adult chronic patients," and "the homeless mentally ill." Good research begins with good conceptualization, including clear and specific operational definitions of terms. Even experienced researchers in this field will be helped to be more clear in their conceptualization by reading Bachrach's provocative piece.

In chapter 3, LeRoy Spaniol and Anthony Zipple describe an area of research that promises to be one of the important lines of work in the field of chronic mental illness: families with mentally ill members. Spaniol and Zipple review needs assessment as well as experimental studies, and show how the findings from each area of research support the others. They cite evidence that many professionals who work with families are unaware of important findings and their implications for practice. One school of thought about practice effectiveness is that the direction of findings about efficacy depends largely upon the degree to which practitioners and their clients agree or disagree about clients' wants or needs. Spaniol and Zipple's chapter supports that thesis.

David Moxley's paper, chapter 4, extends the Spaniol and Zipple thesis, drawing from research on individuals as well as families. Moxley argues that the findings of his research call for a new practice model, one that moves away from an emphasis on psychotherapeutic approaches and toward a resource development approach that includes case management, training and education, rehabilitation and habilitation, and family support. The final chapter in this section, by Wikler and Edwards, illustrates how the research findings and their implications in the field of mental retardation support those in the field of chronic mental illness.

Chapter 1

Review of Current Research on Chronic Mental Illness

Allen Rubin

Substantial progress has occurred over the past 15 years in social work research as well as in other disciplines, on the chronically mentally ill. In the early 1970s, as a doctoral student reviewing literature for a dissertation, I was struck by how little research had been done on the effectiveness of services for the chronically mentally ill. In 1983 the Council on Social Work Education secured funds from the National Institute of Mental Health to assess the state of the art of social work research in mental health. I was asked to conduct that assessment, which was limited to research conducted by social workers during the preceding five years. Of the 16 mental health problem areas identified in that assessment, the social work research enterprise appeared to be strongest in the field of community-based care of the chronically mentally ill (Rubin & Gibelman, 1984).

My assessment of the research cheered me on two counts. First, it contradicted the stereotype of social work research as second-rate compared to the research of other mental health disciplines. Second, the research supported the efficacy of a number of interventions and programs.

The developments of the past 10-15 years in social work research provide ground for optimism. Still, it is hard to discuss what we know in this field without also realizing how much we do *not* know. We still approach a review of the research literature with a caveat in mind: Despite the strides that have been made in recent years, there are significant gaps and limitations in the current research. We still face questions, for example, about the reproducibility of programs tested in completed experiments. And while we discuss what we know, we must also be careful not to foster overgeneralizations and ignore important methodological caveats.

This review does not purport to cover all of the research that has been done on the chronically mentally ill. It is based primarily on the studies I encountered in conducting my earlier assessment for NIMH on the state of social work research. I refer you to that document (Rubin & Gibelman, 1984) for the details of the methodology of that review.

PROBLEMS OF DEFINITION

Before reviewing the research on the chronically mentally ill, one must define who they are. What distinguishes the chronically mental ill from other populations? Years ago, before deinstitutionalization altered our pattern of care for the mentally ill, the term *chronically mentally ill* tended to be reserved for socially disabled persons being discharged after lengthy or multiple institutionalization, persons whose chronicity was thought to be institutionally induced. In the wake of deinstitutionalization, however, the term *chronic* is being applied more loosely. Fewer people are experiencing lengthy institutionalization, and many people who may never be institutionalized are also being labelled as chronically mentally ill.

The Young Adult Chronic Patient

Today the term *young adult chronic patient* is in vogue. The popularity of the term reflects a growing recognition that institutionalization is not a necessary condition of chronicity. The label recognizes further that there is a population of chronic patients whose illnesses were identified in an era of deinstitutionalization and who therefore endure their illnesses outside of protected inpatient environments and receive most of their treatment in outpatient settings (Bachrach, 1982, 1984).

Aside from that recognition, there is little agreement about the specific attributes that distinguish young adult chronic patients from other patients. For example, describing these patients as young connotes age as a distinguishing attribute, but several authors disagree as to the lower and upper age boundaries. And the upper boundary probably expands constantly, as the population of people whose illnesses began in an era of deinstitutionalization grows older. A high degree of residential mobility is often attributed to young adult chronic patients yet the empirical data does not substantiate this notion. In a recent survey of New York State's community support programs, Intagliata and Baker (1984) found as much residential mobility among clients aged 35-54 as among those aged 18-34. Moreover, clients aged 18-34 were actually less mobile than their 18-34 year-old counterparts in the general population. In all older age groups, however, community support system clients were at least twice as likely as their counterparts in the general population to have changed residences within a one-year period.

Young adult chronic patients are often characterized as service refusers. Yet Intagliata and Baker found greater service refusal among chronic clients aged 35-44 than among the younger group. Also, clients aged 35-44 were found to be just as likely as younger clients to abuse alcohol or other drugs, steal property, or threaten to do harm to themselves—additional traits commonly thought to distinguish young adult chronic patients from other chronic patients.

The literature is also unclear about whether a substantial proportion of young adult chronic patients actually have the traits that are thought to distinguish them as a clinical subgroup. Sheets et al. (1982) found, for example, that only 25 percent of young adult chronic patients reported alcohol or drug abuse. Although we may recognize the clinical importance of substance abuse when it does occur among chronic patients, 25 percent is a low rate of incidence for a trait thought to distinguish young adult chronic patients as a subgroup. Moreover, as I already reported, Intagliata and Baker found as much substance abuse among chronic clients aged 35-44 as among the younger ones. They also reported that medication noncompliance and other maladaptive behaviors (such as loss of temper, property damage, and assaultive behavior), while significantly more prevalent among younger patients, "applied to only a very small minority of even the youngest age group." Intagliata and Baker therefore concurred with Sheets et al. in emphasizing the heterogeneity of young adult chronic patients. They added that "we do a disservice to them by stereotyping them according to the most troublesome characteristics of a relatively small minority of their group."

The Intagliata and Baker findings illustrate the uncertainty one encounters in trying to operationally define young adult chronic patients beyond saying, in Leona Bachrach's words, "They are the first generation of chronic psychiatric patients who, since the onset of their illnesses, have lived exclusively in an era of deinstitutionalization" (Bachrach, 1984, p. 573). Bachrach adds that the concept of young adult chronic patients did serve a purpose in raising consciousness about the need to move beyond equating services for the chronically mentally ill with traditional aftercare initiatives for older patients discharged after long-term institutional care.

Diagnosis

Heterogeneity exists not only in connection to the issue of young adult chronic patients but also with regard to diagnosis. People labeled chronically mentally ill, regardless of their age, include those suffering from schizophrenia, affective disorders, paranoid and other psychoses, and personality disorders. There are important differences in these disorders. Schizophrenics, for example, have unique problems connected to the level of expressed emotion that they can tolerate in their families. Likewise, different disorders require different medications that, in turn, produce different side effects.

When reviewing studies, we must be careful to identify which subgroups of the chronically mentally ill specific findings do and do not apply to. Unfortunately, many important studies do not provide enough specificity regarding their samples or their definitions of chronicity to indicate appropriate boundaries of external validity. For example, many studies that evaluate alternatives to institutional care for clients requiring hospital admission lump together first admissions, acute cases, chronic cases, or cases that are unspecified regarding chronicity or diagnosis. When such studies support the efficacy of community-based alternative care, it may not be clear whether successful outcomes would have been attained had all the clients been clearly chronic. Moreover, some of these studies were carried out at a time when the criteria for admission to psychiatric hospital may have been less stringent than they are now. Consequently, patients currently deemed to require institutionalization, particularly those whose disabilities are chronic, clearly may be more disturbed than the ones in earlier studies (Braun et al., 1981). In addition, some studies cream patients before randomization to experimental and control conditions, perhaps excluding patients without families willing to live with them, violent or criminal or suicidal patients, extremely young or old patients, and so on (Bachrach, 1980, 1982a; Braun et al., 1981; Kiesler, 1982). Consequently, generalizations from such studies to the broad rubric of the chronically mentally ill would be precarious, despite the fact that these studies deal with *deinstitutionalization*—a term that tends to be associated with the *chronically* mentally ill.

Chronicity

A further problem lies in the difficulty of defining *chronicity*. The task was simpler when chronicity was largely equated with duration of institutional stay, but that criterion is not sufficient in an era of deinstitutionalization. One approach has been to use social disability as an indicator of chronicity. Yet the term *social disability* itself lacks operational specificity—at least in terms that we could all agree on. For example, at a recent conference in Texas on the chronically mentally ill, Pepper (1984) defined a socially disabled person as one who has been dysfunctional for at least two years in any one of three areas: work or school, family, or social relationships. (Members of the audience responded that this definition could apply to the staff of treatment programs as well as to their clients.) Others describe social disability in terms of social isolation, a high degree of vulnerability to stress, extreme dependency, deficiencies in coping skills, difficulty with interpersonal relationships, and difficulties with the basic activities of daily living. But there is little precision about the intensity and extent of those attributes that must be present before we can separate the chronically mentally ill from others. Without such precision, in Leona Bachrach's (1984) words, "we run a serious risk of lumping individuals with severe and unremitting psychopathology together with what one journalist calls 'confused relics of the drug culture'" (p. 577). There is, again, substantial diversity in the degree of social disability among patients whom the literature has defined as chronically mentally ill. These patients include those who live with their families as well as homeless persons whom Segal and Baumohl (1980) call "street people" or whom others call "the new drifters" (Lamb, 1982). The chronically mentally ill include patients who eventually can make substantial progress in social and vocational functioning as well as those who, even with long-term rehabilitative treatment, cannot meet the simple demands of everyday living (Lamb and Peele, 1984).

A Working Definition

In view of all the heterogeneity, disagreement, and ambiguity that I have been discussing, what definition of chronic mental illness should guide a review of the research on the chronically mentally ill? A sound, if not ideal, approach is provided by Leona Bachrach, who suggests that we can best approximate the concept of the chronically mentally ill person as "one who has a severe and persistent psychiatric disorder that will render him or her dependent on psychiatric and support services for a very long time—often, if not usually, for life" (Bachrach, 1984, p. 577). Put another way, Bachrach defines chronicity "to include all persons who are, have been, or might have been but for the deinstitutionalization movement, on the rolls of long-term mental institutions, especially state hospitals" (1983, p. 10). In line with this approach, I selected research studies for my review if they met any one of three criteria:

1. Claimed to be about the chronically mentally ill (in the title, sample description, and so on).
2. Assessed services that offered long-term institutional care or that were designed as alternatives to such care.
3. Assessed subjects with histories of prior psychiatric hospitalizations.

Using the above criteria meant including in the review studies on patients deemed admittable to inpatient care who, on average, spent more than a year in prior psychiatric institutionalization. But it meant excluding studies, such as the one by Mosher and Menn (1978) on Soteria House, which evaluated community-based alternatives to hospitalization for newly admitted patients, almost all of whom were experiencing their first episode of schizophrenia, and which did not depict clients as chronic.

OUTCOME STUDIES

My review of outcome studies excludes physiologically oriented studies of chemotherapy, studies reported more than 10 years ago, and studies that were incomplete from the standpoint of experimental design. For example, group experiments that failed to utilize random assignment were excluded. However, two single-subject experiments with adequate internal validity due to multiple baseline conditions and reliable measurement were included. The outcome studies fell into several categories, according to the type of patients, program, or intervention assessed:

1. Varied aftercare services
2. Foster care
3. Day treatment in the aftercare of schizophrenics
4. Drugs and sociotherapy in aftercare for schizophrenics
5. Intervention with families of schizophrenic patients
6. Social skills training
7. Comprehensive community care

Only one study was identified in each of the first three categories (varied aftercare, foster care, and day treatment). Most of the findings in each study favored, on balance, the efficacy of the experimental treatment, although they were somewhat equivocal and not entirely conclusive (Weinman and Kleiner, 1978; Linn et al., 1977; Linn et al., 1979).

The fourth category of study, a long-range series of experiments by Hogarty (1979) and his associates on drugs and sociotherapy, also had results that were somewhat equivocal, indicating that sociotherapy combined with chemotherapy might be effective in forestalling relapse for discharged schizophrenic patients who survive the first six months of discharge. The sociotherapy was called "major role therapy." It was administered by experienced MSWs and emphasized a problem-solving casework focusing on vocational or homemaking functions, interpersonal interactions, monitoring of medication maintenance, provision of material resources (financial assistance and housing), and self-care skills.

Most of the above studies produced an important finding about the circumstances under which the tested interventions had negative effects for some patients. Foster homes with negative outcomes for schizophrenic patients, for example, appeared to be distinguished by excessive environmental stimulation (Linn et al., 1977). Likewise, day treatment centers with the poorest results provided more intensive psychotherapeutic treatment; those with the best results provided more occupational therapy (Linn et al., 1977). Patients with symptoms of motor retardation, emotional withdrawal, and anxiety seemed unable to tolerate the overstimulation in the centers offering more intensive psychotherapeutic treatment.

Interpretation was offered in the experiments on major role therapy conducted by Hogarty and his associates. When it was combined with a placebo instead of chemotherapy, major role therapy resulted in greater relapse than did the placebo alone. Also, schizophrenic patients with the worst symptomatology were unable to cope, even when they received chemotherapy, with the overstimulating therapeutic environment. Hogarty (1979) therefore concluded that one of the most accurate predictors of relapse was the degree of conflict in a patient's home prior to treatment.

Intervention with Families

These negative findings regarding the vulnerability of some schizophrenics to overstimulating environments, unrealistic expectations, and family conflict are closely connected to the fifth category of outcome studies, on intervention with families of schizophrenic patients. A series of British studies established a strong correlation between the level of expressed emotion (EE) shown by relatives and the outcome of schizophrenia in patients living with them. Specifically, relapse is more likely if relatives are excessively critical or overinvolved with the schizophrenic patient. Statistical analysis of data from some of the studies suggested that drug therapy and reduction of face-to-face contact between patient and relatives had additive effects in protecting from relapse. Statistical analysis also undermined the possibility that the relatives' high EE was a function of the patients' disturbed behavior (Leff, 1976).

Falloon et al. (1982) reported a similar experiment with favorable results in which previously hospitalized schizophrenics deemed to have a high risk of relapse and living primarily with high EE relatives were randomly assigned to two treatment groups. One group received drug therapy plus family intervention geared to teaching patients and their parents how to reduce environmental stress. The intervention educated them about schizophrenia and refuted the notion that families cause it, but acknowledged that the family can play a role in improving the course of the illness. It also included discussion and skills-training sessions to reduce existing tensions and improve skills for coping with causes of stress. The comparison group received drug therapy and individual aftercare counseling in "the best available...well-staffed community after-care clinics." The comparison group also received an education component similar to the one in the family intervention, but it was delivered only to the patient. Strong, statistically significant differences favoring the family intervention group were found on almost all measures of outcome, including symptomatology (as judged by blind raters) and hospital readmissions.

Hogarty and his associates are currently evaluating a similar package of family intervention called a "psychoeducational" approach. Although they report that the preliminary, impressionistic results of this research on this approach look encouraging, the outcome data haven't yet been reported (Anderson et al., 1980).

One additional outcome study bears noting, although it does not meet the criteria for inclusion in this review. Vaughn et al. (1984) replicated the British findings on expressed emotion and found that criticism and overinvolvement expressed by a key relative about the patient at time of admission proved to be the best predictor of symptomatic relapse after hospital discharge. Clearly, this is a fertile and promising area for future outcome research. We must remember that the point of these interventions is not always to reduce the social stimulation and expectations to which schizophrenic patients are exposed. Rather, the point is to reduce *excessive* stimulation and pressure, "balancing the need for some social relationships on the one hand with the need to avoid a noxious level of emotional intensity on the other" (Budson, 1983, p. 531). In other words, social understimulation must also be avoided, for studies have also shown that too little social stimulation can exacerbate already present tendencies toward social withdrawal among schizophrenic patients (Wing, 1978).

Social Skills Training

Another important body of research has assessed the outcome of social skills training for chronic mental patients. An interesting thing about this intervention is that its efficacy has been supported in both group and single-subject experiments. In a group experiment, Bellack et al. (1984) provided evidence that six months after treatment had ended, chronic schizophrenic patients who received social skill training and day hospital treatment did better than day hospital controls on measures of symptomatology and social functioning. Earlier, Herson and Bellack (1979) reported favorable results for such training in a multiple-baseline study (across assertive target behaviors) of two chronic schizophrenic patients. In a multiple-baseline study on six chronic schizophrenic patients in a day treatment program,

Kelly et al. (1979) reported evidence supporting the efficacy of a group training procedure to teach job interviewing skills.

Comprehensive Community Care

In their review of studies on psychosocial treatments for schizophrenia, Mosher and Keith (1981) concluded that the most effective treatments were those providing the most comprehensive, corrective, and sustaining social support systems. In a somewhat similar conclusion, Braun et al. (1981) observed in their review of deinstitutionalization research that although experimental studies provide some support for the efficacy of community-based alternatives to psychiatric hospitalization, satisfactory deinstitutionalization appears to depend on the availability of these diverse programs in the community. Likewise, Keisler (1982) concludes his otherwise positive review of deinstitutionalization outcome studies by noting that one cannot infer that they are applicable over the range of problems among people ordinarily institutionalized. In view of the multifaceted needs of the chronically mentally ill and the diverse diagnostic categories lumped under the rubric of chronic mental illness, perhaps the most important studies are those assessing comprehensive programs of community care. These programs attempt to provide an array of services that address the full range of needs of chronic patients in the community.

One of the most renowned and exemplary studies of comprehensive community support, reported by Stein and Test (1980), evaluated a program called "training in community living" (TCL). Patients with a mean of 14.6 months of previous psychiatric hospitalization were randomly assigned to a hospitalized control group or to the TCL program. The TCL program included ten components:

1. Residential resources: independent rooms and apartments in the community.
2. Pharmacotherapy.
3. Full schedule of daily activities.
4. In vivo teaching of coping skills.

5. In vivo teaching, encouragement, and assistance in basic living skills (e.g., laundry, grooming, budgeting, shopping, cooking, using public transportation).
6. Employment services (e.g., assistance in finding a job or sheltered workshop placement, and daily staff contact with patients, supervisors and employers for on-the-job problem solving).
7. Staff support for involvement in community recreation and social activities in order to use leisure time constructively and develop social skills, frequently including initial accompaniment by staff to such functions until patients felt comfortable enough to attend by themselves.
8. Work with families (entitled "constructive separation") to regulate interactions with patient by parents, parental surrogates, or siblings with whom patient is in a pathological relationship (including staff reassurance and guidance).
9. Work with the community to encourage key community figures (such as police and landlords) to talk to patients about their behavior, to point out the consequences of patients' behavior as if they were ordinary citizens (eviction or jail, not return to hospital), and to call staff at any time for help.
10. Unique staffing attributes, including:
    a. Retraining and moving an entire inpatient unit staff to the community.
    b. Ensuring that staff have experience with, and commitment to, the target population and a service orientation that includes a case management approach to practice, including working with patients in their homes and neighborhoods, helping patients secure material resources (food, shelter, clothing, medical care), and assertive perseverance and outreach to promote appropriate medication and compliance with other treatment components.

The outcome of the TCL experiment favored the TCL group in terms of hospital readmissions and time spent in independent settings, time spent unemployed, amount of interpersonal contact, life satisfaction, and symptomatology. However, once patients were weaned from the TCL program and integrated into traditional community programs, most of the differences disappeared. Stein and Test concluded that this result supported the efficacy of the TCL approach "as an ongoing rather than time-limited endeavor."

Although other studies have utilized experimental or credible quasi-experimental designs to evaluate the outcome of community-based alternatives to hospital admission, the work of Stein and Test is the most exemplary of these studies. Whereas other studies also had findings favoring the community-based programs they evaluated, the Stein and Test study stands out from the others in several respects:

- Comprehensiveness of the services provided.
- Absence of potential bias in how patients were allocated to experimental and control groups.
- Not restricting the sample to patients living at home with their own families or to those without a history of chronicity, and not failing to state explicity their selection/exclusion criteria.
- Use, as a control condition, of a reputable hospital that offered a high staff-to-patient ratio as well as partial hospitalization and aftercare (as opposed to using a control condition of unspecified or dubious quality).
- Assessing the burden to the family for those patients whose families lived nearby (with results suggesting no greater burden for experimental patients).
- Assessing the cost-benefit of the program (with results, given a number of assumptions and approximations, suggesting a small net benefit for the alternative care group).

But, despite these advantages, the Stein and Test study, like other studies in the area, is not immune to a number of concerns that have been voiced, particularly regarding external validity. Bachrach (1980) has argued that such programs may not be reproducible or appropriate in other communities. Would other localities allocate public expenditures for these comprehensive programs? Another issue is the comprehensiveness of these programs: while a strength from one perspective, it can pose a problem in sorting out the aspects of the program most responsible for the favorable outcome. Test and Stein (1978) have acknowledged this problem, admitting that beyond some basic principles they do not know what makes these comprehensive programs effective.

Studies of comprehensive community programs commonly fail to indicate whether or not raters on several dependent variables were blind as to experimental conditions (Braun et al., 1981; Straw, 1983). (The issue of lack of blindness in rating outcomes appears to be a problem across a number of studies in this area.) In his meta-analysis of deinstitutionalization outcome studies, Straw (1983) noted that studies that were ambiguous regarding the blinding of assessors found stronger effect sizes for the experimental programs than did studies that were explicit about the blinding of the assessors. Perhaps a bigger issue than potential measurement bias, however, is the rather large vulnerability these studies have to biases in the readmission data connected to the ideologies or commitments of their staff. If the personnel in special demonstration projects attempting to provide alternatives to institutional care tend to value the notion of avoiding hospitalization whenever possible, then they may be averse to recommending hospitalization for their experimental-group patients. In contrast, mental health personnel in the same locale, but not associated with the demonstration projects, may be more prone to recommend hospitalization for comparison group patients functioning at the same level as the experimental patients. If so, this bias may account for the observed differences in readmission rates in various studies. A related bias would be the knowledge by program personnel that the success of their program would be determined in large part by rehospitalization rates.

Even if staff biases do not obviate the internal validity of these studies, they create much doubt about their external validity. For example, some researchers maintain that these demonstration projects attract enthusiastic practitioners who are already devoted to the care of the chronically mentally ill (Bachrach, 1980; Braun et al., 1981) and that enthusiasm is fostered by a "Hawthorne effect," making it difficult to distinguish the planned programmatic effects from those effects resulting from "the mere fact of participating in an experiment" (Bachrach, 1980, p. 1027). Therefore, it seems reasonable to assume that programs that were evaluated under relatively ideal conditions in terms of funding, staffing, and practitioner zeal might not yield such favorable results if adopted in other communities where they may have inadequate funding, poor interagency coordination, weak practitioner commitment, and less community support (Bachrach, 1980). Of course, this skepticism applies to the whole gamut of experimental outcome studies.

SERVICE DELIVERY STUDIES

Skepticism about how successfully the foregoing programs have been implemented in other settings is supported by an abundance of evidence. Utilizing survey or qualitative methods, several studies have documented:

- insufficiencies in the range of services currently available for the chronically mentally ill in many communities (Bachrach, 1980a; Morrissey & Goldman, 1984; Solomon et al., 1980);
- inadequacies in the services that *do* exist (for example, relative neglect in some community-based residential alternatives or inhumane conditions in shelters for the homeless mentally ill) (Baxter & Hopper, 1982; Kinard, 1981);
- obstacles to engaging many young chronically mentally ill patients in coordinated community services (Segal & Baumohl, 1980);
- community opposition to the establishment of alternative-care programs (Johnson, 1980; Johnson & Beditz, 1981; Davidson, 1982; Solomon, 1983; Segal, Baumohl & Moyles, 1980);
- negative attitudes by community mental health practitioners toward the chronically mentally ill or toward various interventions implied by a rehabilitative approach to service with this population that contrast with a more psychotherapeutic, or "curative," approach to clients who have

been called "healthy but unhappy" or "the worried well" (Hogarty, 1971; Lamb, 1979; Rubin & Johnson, 1982; Menninger, 1984; Rubin, 1978; Sherman & Newman, 1979.

This skepticism is intensified by the observation that the favorable effects of the experimental programs tend to be maintained only as long as patients remain active in them; positive results tend to reverse after patients are weaned from the programs. This observation supports the internal validity of these studies—that is, desirable outcomes appear only when the independent variable is in effect, and undesirable outcomes appear once it is withdrawn. But how much enthusiasm can we anticipate from communities that already assign low priority to the chronically mentally ill when they are asked to finance programs that must be prolonged indefinitely with most patients in order to sustain their effects—effects that may be deemed modest by individuals who envision more dramatic "cures" for acute problems?

NEED TO STUDY INSTITUTIONAL AND RESIDENTIAL CARE

In light of the problems in service delivery to the deinstitutionalized mentally ill, it is relevant to ask also about the functions performed by traditional institutions. In this day of deinstitutionalization, little research is being conducted on the quality of institutional care. An implicit bias seems to prevail in research: the question "What works?" applies only to community-based programs, not to institutions. Researchers tend to see institutions only as comparison groups, without recognizing the diversity in the quality of institutional care and without bothering to inquire about outcomes that might be achieved if resources allocated to models of community-based care were allocated instead to upgrading institutional care.

In view of the research on the plight of the chronically mentally ill in more typical communities that don't have enthusiastic practitioners providing model programs offering a comprehensive range of appropriate community-based services for the chronically mentally ill, and which are unlikely to experience community support for the creation of such programs, some authors are postulating functions that traditional institutions might perform better than the "average" community-based system of care that assigns priority to the "healthy but unhappy" and neglects the chronically mentally ill (Bachrach, 1983). Likewise, research on schizophrenia as well as on the emergence of young adult chronic patients who never experienced lengthy institutionalization indicates that the social disabilities of chronic patients cannot be attributed merely to institutionalism. Consequently, some authors are discussing the need for continuing asylum and sanctuary and the need to ensure the performance of such functions as removing patients from pathogenic environmental influences, protecting them from exploitation, providing them with respite from mounting pressures, and so on (Bachrach, 1983; Lamb & Peele, 1984).

Special acknowledgment must be given to the small amount of research being done on institutional care or on residential facilities that provide asylum in community-based settings. Studies by Tom Holland, Claudia Coulton, and their associates at Case Western Reserve University report the development of scales to assess staff and patient participation in decisions about treatment planning and routine patient care. These scales, which measure a continuum of inpatient unit orientations, assess relationships between institutional structure and resident outcomes. The team of researchers found improved potential for community adjustment in wards with more individualized care, more satisfied staff, and greater staff and resident participation in treatment planning (Petchers-Cassell & Holland, 1979; Holland et al., 1981; Smith & Holland, 1982; Buffum & Konick, 1982). In a recent study, Coulton et al. (1985) identified four types of social environments in community care homes:

- Homes that were basically shelters with minimal organized programming, structure, and social involvement;
- Homes with some structured programming but few socioemotional resources or demands;
- Homes with little structured programming but relatively

high focus on socioemotional concerns and expectations;
- Homes that emphasize both high structure and socio-emotional concerns.

The Coulton study is intriguing for two reasons: first, it addresses the often neglected diversity in chronic patients and the need to individualize their care—in this case, in regard to the type of social environment the patients can best tolerate and adapt to; second, it illustrates in operational terms how the social work concept of person-in-environment can be implemented in matching the needs and capabilities of the chronic patient to the appropriate residential environment.

The foregoing studies have spawned other studies, such as one by Kruzich and Kruzich (1985) on the milieu factors and patient-functioning factors that influence patient integration into community residential facilities. However, the paucity of such studies is striking; with a few exceptions, it is remarkable how little residential and institutional care is being studied. One exception is a study by Shadish and Bootzin (1984) that assesses the nature of nursing home care for the chronically mentally ill. They found it custodial and institutional, yet fitting the needs and capacities of most chronic mental patients placed in nursing homes.

It bears repeating that although the average patient in outcome studies such as that by Stein and Test (1980) may have had a little over a year of prior hospitalization, many patients had less. The favorable results of outcome studies cannot be generalized indiscriminantly to all chronic patients. Although such services may be ideal for many chronic patients, other patients are more regressed, and perhaps violent, and may require longer-term care in protective environments. It seems that the neglect of these individuals in programs of care is paralleled by neglect of them in research on that care.

EMERGING AREAS OF RESEARCH

It is important to acknowledge some other important areas of inquiry. One hot topic these days is research on the homeless mentally ill. A group of NIMH-supported studies are underway, designed to investigate service needs among the homeless mentally ill in a variety of settings. In discussing research on service, I have alluded to several studies documenting the inhumane conditions in shelters for the homeless mentally ill, obstacles to engaging the homeless mentally ill in coordinated community services, and opposition by community residents to the social integration of shelter residents into their neighborhoods. Among the most prominent and frequently cited of these studies is a series of qualitative and quantitative investigations reported by Steven Segal and his associates (Segal & Baumohl, 1980; Segal, Baumohl & Moyles, 1980; Segal, 1981).

The growing concern about young adult chronic patients is also related to homelessness. Phyllis Solomon and her associates (1984a) recently reported a needs assessment of discharged chronic psychiatric patients, an assessment that they connected to the recent awareness of the heterogeneity of the chronically mentally ill in the wake of deinstitutionalization, and to the diversity of needs among the maturing "baby-boom generation." Their findings emphasized the need for substance-abuse counseling for young adult chronic patients who are exposed to the ready availability of street drugs and alcohol in the community and who are hypersensitive to the use of those substances. They also emphasized the need for vocational rehabilitation services for these young patients, who are often able-bodied and may still have life goals.

In another important study related to the multiplicity and diversity of needs of chronic aftercare patients, Solomon and her associates (1984b) utilized sophisticated statistical controls in the tracking of a cohort of discharged state hospital patients, to isolate those factors that differentiated readmissions from those not readmitted. Although they found no significant difference in readmission between aftercare service receivers and non-receivers, the two most significant predictors of readmission were the number of different types of services received and the extent to which patients received the services that they were assessed as needing. By going further than merely looking at the utilization of aftercare services and by examining the variety and relevance of the aftercare services utilized, Solomon and her associates have provided a plausible hypothesis that might help explain why earlier multivariate analyses in this area, including those by such social work researchers as Elane Neuhring (1980) and her associates and by Stuart Kirk (1976), have yielded inconsistent results.

CONCLUSION

In closing, I am excited about how far we have come in this field of research. But we still have a long way to go, not only in filling the gaps in the research but also—for those of us who are social work educators—in exciting our students about this field. Peter Johnson and I (Rubin & Johnson, 1984) recently reported a study indicating that most MSW students today aspire to a private practice with the "healthy but unhappy" and view the chronically mentally ill as an unappealing clientele to work with. We have sufficient scientific evidence for optimism about the potential efficacy of work with the chronically mentally ill. If social workers are enthusiastic about working in this field, they can know that there is substantial and sound, albeit incomplete, empirical support for some interventions. Dissemination of the research reviewed in this paper will enable us to stir more enthusiasm in this field among both faculty and students.

REFERENCES

Anderson, C., Hogarty, G., & Reiss, D. (1980). Family treatment of adult schizophrenic patients: A psychoeducational approach. *Schizophrenia Bulletin, 6,* 490-502.

Bachrach, L. (1980a). Is the least restrictive environment always the best? Sociological and semantic implications. *Hospital and Community Psychiatry, 31*(2), 97-103.

Bachrach, L. (1980b). Overview: Model programs for chronic mental patients. *American Journal of Psychiatry, 137*(9), 1023-1031.

Bachrach, L. (1982a). Assessment of outcome in community support systems: Results, problems and limitations, *Schizophrenia Bulletin, 8*(1), 39-61.

Bachrach, L. (1982b). Young adult chronic patients: An analytical review of the literature. *Hospital and Community Psychiatry, 33*(3), 189-197.

Bachrach, L. (1983). Concepts and issues in deinstitutionalization. In I. Barofsky & R.D. Budson (Eds.), *The chronic psychiatric patient in the community*. New York: SP Medical & Scientific Books, 5-28.

Bachrach, L. (1984). The concept of young adult chronic psychiatric patients: Questions from a research perspective. *Hospital and Community Psychiatry, 35*(6), 573-580.

Barofsky, I. (1983). Community survival of the chronic psychiatric patient: Research priorities. In I. Barofsky & R.D. Budson (Eds.), *The chronic psychiatric patient in the community*. New York: SP Medical and Scientific Books, 541-561.

Baxter, E. & Hopper, K. (1982). The new mendicancy: Homeless in New York City. *American Journal of Orthopsychiatry, 52,* 393-407.

Bellack, A., Turner, S., Hersen, M., & Luber, R. (1984). An examination of the efficacy of social skills training for chronic schizophrenic patients. *Hospital and Community Psychiatry, 35*(10), 1023-1028.

Berkowitz, R., Everlein-Fries, R., Kuipers, L., & Leff, J. (1984). Educating relatives about schizophrenia. *Schizophrenia Bulletin, 10*(3), 418-429.

Braun, P., Kochansky, G., Shapiro, R., Greenberg, S., Gudeman, J., Johnson, S., & Shore, M. (1981). Overview: Deinstitutionalization of psychiatric patients, a critical review of outcome studies. *American Journal of Psychiatry, 138*(6), 736-749.

Budson, R. (1983). Essential principles in the delivery of adequate clinical care to the chronic psychiatric patient in the community. In I. Barofsky & R.D. Budson (Eds.), *The chronic psychiatric patient in the community*. New York: SP Medical and Scientific Books, 527-540.

Buffman, W. & Konick, A. (1982). Employees' job satisfaction, residents' functioning, and treatment progress in psychiatric institutions. *Health and Social Work, 7*(4), 320-327.

Coulton, C., Fitch, V., & Holland, T. (1985). A typology of social environments in community care homes. *Hospital and Community Psychiatry, 36*(4), 373-377.

Davidson, J. (1982). Balancing required resources and neighborhood opposition in community-based treatment center neighborhoods. *Social Service Review,* 55-69.

Falloon, R., Boyd, J., McGill, C., Razani, J., Moss, H., & Gilderman, A. (1982). Family management in the prevention of exacerbations of schizophrenia: A controlled study. *The New England Journal of Medicine, 306*(24), 1437-1440.

Fisher, J. (1973). Is casework effective: A review. *Social Work,* 1973, 5-20.

Hersen, M. & Bellack, A. (1976). A multiple-baseline analysis of social skills training in chronic schizophrenics. *Journal of Applied Behavior Analysis, 9*(3), 239-245.

Hogarty, G. (1971). The plight of schizophrenics in modern treatment programs. *Hospital and Community Psychiatry, 22*(7), 197-203.

Hogarty, G. (1979). Aftercare treatment of schizophrenia: Current status and future direction. In H.M. Pragg (Ed.), *Management of schizophrenia*. Assen, The Netherlands: Van Gorcum, 19-36.

Holland, T., Konick, A., Buffum, W., Smith, M., & Petchers, M. (1981). Institutional structure and resident outcomes. *Journal of Health and Social Behavior, 22,* 433-444.

Intagliata, J. & Baker, F. (1984). A comparative analysis of the young adult chronic patient in New York State's community support system. *Hospital and Community Psychiatry, 35*(1), 45-50.

Johnson, P. (1980). The input of community acceptance in an open systems process model of community support systems for the chronically mentally ill. *Community Support Service Journal, 4,* 6-11.

Johnson, P. & Beditz, J. (1981). Community support systems scaling community acceptance. *Community Mental Health Journal, 17,* 153-160.

Kelly, J., Laughlin, C., Claiborne, M., & Patterson, J. (1979). A group procedure for teaching job interviewing skills to formerly hospitalized psychiatric patients. *Behavior Therapy, 10,* 299-310.

Kiesler, C. (1982). Mental hospitals and alternative care: Noninstitutionalization as potential public policy, *American Psychologist, 37*(4), 349-360.

Kinard, E.M. (1981). Discharged patients who desire to return to the hospital. *Hospital and Community Psychiatry, 32,* 194-197.

Kirk, S. (1976). Effectiveness of community services for discharged mental hospital patients. *American Journal of Orthopsychiatry, 46,* 646-659.

Kruzich, J.M. & Kruzich, J.J. (1985). Milieu factors influencing patients' integration into community residential facilities. *Hospital and Community Psychiatry, 36*(4), 378-382.

Lamb, H.R. (1979). Staff burnout in work with long-term patients. *Hospital and Community Psychiatry, 30*(6), 396-398.

Lamb, H. (1982). Young adult chronic patients: The new drifters. *Hospital and Community Psychiatry, 33,* 465-468.

Lamb, H. & Peele, R. (1984). The need for continuing asylum and sanctuary. *Hospital and Community Psychiatry, 35*(8), 798-802.

Leff, J. (1976). Schizophrenia and sensitivity to the family environment. *Schizophrenia Bulletin, 2,* 566-574.

Leff, J., Kuipers, L., Berkowitz, R., Eberlein-Vries, R., & Sturgeon, D. (1982). A controlled trial of social intervention in the families of schizophrenic patients. *British Journal of Psychiatry, 141,* 121-134.

Linn, M., Caffey, E., Klett, C., & Hogarty, G. (1977). Hospital vs. community (foster) care for psychiatric patients. *Archives of General Psychiatry, 34,* 78-83.

Linn, M., Caffey, E., Klett, C., Hogarty, G., & Lamb, H. (1979). Day treatment and psychotropic drugs in the aftercare of schizophrenic patients. *Archives of General Psychiatry, 36,* 1055-1066.

Menninger, W. (1984). Dealing with staff reactions to perceived lack of progress by chronic mental patients. *Hospital and Community Psychiatry, 35*(8), 805-808.

Morrissey, J. & Goldman, H. (1984). Cycles of reform in the care of the chronically mentally ill. *Hospital and Community Psychiatry, 35*(8), 785-793.

Mosher, L. & Keith, S. (1980). Psychosocial treatment: Individual, group, family, and community support approaches. In National Institute of Mental Health, *Special Report: Schizophrenia,* (DH HS#ADM 81-1064).

Mosher L. & Menn, A. (1978). Community residential treatment for schizophrenia: Two-year follow-up. *Hospital and community psychiatry, 29,* 715-723.

Neuhring, E., Thayer, J., & Lander, R. (1980). On the factors predicting rehospitalization among two state mental hospital populations. *Administration in Mental Health, 7,* 247-270.

Pepper, B. (1985). Conference presentation: Treating the young adult chronic patient: Approaches and dilemmas. Sponsored by the Texas Department of MHMR and ATC-MHMR, Austin, Texas.

Petchers-Cassell, M. & Holland, T. (1979). Staff and patients participation in decision making in residential treatment programs. *Social Work Research and Abstracts, 15*(4), 37-44.

Rubin, A. (1978). Commitment to community mental health aftercare services: Staffing and structural implications. *Community Mental Health Journal, 14,* 199-208.

Rubin, R. & Gibelman, M. (1984). *Social work research in mental health: The state of the art.* National Institute of Mental Health.

Rubin, A. & Johnson, P. (1982). Practitioner orientations toward serving the chronically disabled: Prospects for policy implementation. *Administration in Mental Health, 10*(3), 2-12.

Rubin, A. & Johnson, P. (1984). Direct practice interests of entering MSW students. *Journal of Education for Social Work, 20*(2), 5-16.

Segal, S. & Baumohl, J. (1980). Engaging the disengaged: Proposals on madness and vagrancy. *Social Work, 25,* 358-365.

Segal, S., Baumohl, J., & Moyles, E. (1980). Neighborhood types and community reaction to the mentally ill: A paradox of intensity. *Journal of Health and Social Behavior, 21,* 345-359.

Segal, S. (1981). The impact of recent rehospitalization on community adjustment. *International Journal of Social Psychiatry, 27,* 163-172.

Shadish, W., Jr. & Bootzin, R. (1984). The social integration of psychiatric patients in nursing homes. *American Journal of Psychiatry, 141*(10), 1203-1207.

Sheets, J., Prevost, J., & Reihman, J. (1982). Young adult chronic patients: Three hypothesized sub-groups. *Hospital and Community Psychiatry, 33*(3), 197-203.

Sherman, S. & Newman, E. (1979). Role of the caseworker in adult foster care. *Social Work, 24,* 324-328.

Smith, M. & Holland, T. (1982). Measurement of institutional resident management practices. *Journal of Social Service Research, 6*(1/2), 17-29.

Solomon, E. et al. (1980). Assessing the community care of chronic psychotic patients. *Hospital and Community Psychiatry, 31,* 113-116.

Solomon, P. (1983). Analyzing opposition to community residential facilities for troubled adolescents. *Child Welfare, 62,* 361-366.

Solomon, P., Gordon, B., & Davis, J. (1984a). Assessing the service needs of the discharged psychiatric patient. *Social Work in Health Care, 10*(1), 61-69.

Solomon P., Gordon, B., & Davis, J., (1984b). Differentiating psychiatric readmissions from non-readmissions. *American Journal of Orthopsychiatry, 34*(3), 426-435.

Stein, L. & Test, M. (1980). Alternative to mental hospital treatment: I. Conceptual model, treatment program and clinical evaluation. *Archives of General Psychiatry, 37,* 392-397.

Straw, R. (1983). Deinstitutionalization in mental health: A meta-analysis. *Evaluation Studies Review Annual,* 253-278.

Test, M. & Stein, L. (1978). Training in community living: Research design and results. In Stein and Test (Eds.), *Alternatives to mental hospital treatment.* New York: Plenum.

Vaughn, C., Snyder, K., Jones, S., Freeman, W., & Falloon, I. (1984). Family factors in schizophrenic relapse. *Archives of General Psychiatry, 41,* 1169-1177.

Weinman, B. & Kleiner, R. (1978). The impact of community living and community member intervention on the adjustment of the chronic psychotic patient. In L.I. Stein and M.A. Test (Eds.), *Alternative to mental hospital treatment.* New York: Plenum Press.

Wing, J. (1978). The social context of schizophrenia. *American Journal of Psychiatry, 135*(1), 1333-1339.

Chapter 2

Conceptual Issues: The Questions that Precede the Research Questions

Leona L. Bachrach

A long time ago—back in the years when I was doing housewifely kinds of things—I had an opportunity to observe at very close hand the planning and execution of a large study of ischemic heart disease among Israeli civil servants. I myself was not directly involved in that study, but my husband was the Project Director representing the National Institutes of Health, which was conducting the research under something called P.L. 480 funds—an arrangement by which foreign governments could pay off their debts to the United States by contracting out research opportunities.

The Israeli heart disease study was a comprehensive epidemiological inquiry of multivariate design. A wide array of physiological, sociological, demographic, nutritional, and psychological factors were being investigated for their relationship to heart disease. You'll remember, of course, that 20 or 25 years ago, Israel provided a kind of natural laboratory for studying those kinds of things—because almost everyone who lived there had come from some other place; and national heritages, dietary and health practices, and other cultural patterns were still very much intact.

Now, the Israeli and American scientists who organized this investigation used a battery of research instruments—including a psychological status questionnaire that asked, among other things, the question, "Are you happy with your wife?" And, when the study results began to come in, the investigators found—much to their surprise—that this seemingly simple question had backfired. Some of the respondents had answered, "Which wife?" What had happened was that the study's designers had forgotten—or else they had never known—that new immigrants to Israel who had contracted polygamous marriages in their countries of origin were being permitted to keep those marriages intact, although new polygamous unions were forbidden. And, what's more, the difficulties that this question generated didn't even surface during the carefully conducted pilot runs.

So far as I am concerned, these are problems that need to be dealt with before we can even begin to do anything that approaches relevant research. And, if they can't be dealt with, they at least need to be recognized—and some compensation should be made for them.

In short, I want to address some of the questions that precede the research questions.

What I'm going to do this morning, then—with that end in mind—is focus on two major areas of research in our field today—young adult chronic patients and the homeless mentally ill. I've selected these two research areas for a couple of reasons that I'll share with you. First of all, concern with these two subpopulations of the chronically mentally ill is very timely. These groupings somehow epitomize the problems of service delivery that we're encountering in today's mental health service systems, and there's widespread interest in them.

But, even beyond this, I've decided to concentrate on these two subpopulations for another reason. Not only are they of timely concern; but they seem to throw the major conceptual and methodological difficulties that are general to our field into bold relief.

But I want to make a couple of digressions even before I begin. One of these digressions is brief. It concerns some of my own biases that I want to make explicit.

Since a lot of what I'm going to be talking about this morning has a semantic dimension—and since I'm going to have quite a lot to say about semantics in general—I think that it's only fair for me to share with you my own verbal biases and sort of get that out of the way. So I want to confess to you that—maybe as a byproduct of my own history of physical illness—I experience some uneasiness when the word "client" is substituted for the word "patient." John Talbott (1984), the immediate past president of the American Psychiatric Association, has a similar reaction, and he's recently written about this.

Talbott explains that to be a patient is also to gain access to certain benefits that aren't available to people who are regarded as clients. We can think of these benefits, if we want to, as entitlements—although I think that the term entitlement itself has distinct monetary connotations (Ehrenreich, 1982), and I'm referring now to concerns that are really more qualitative in nature.

The late Franz Ingelfinger (1980) made an eloquent statement on this subject. He perceived, and wrote about, the world as both a terminally ill patient and a renowned physician. He held that people who are sick already have enough to deal with, without having to expend energy on seeking their own boundaries—and that the patient designation has implicit in it a certain amount of comfort. Only after he had accepted his own patient identity, Ingelfinger wrote, was he able to mobilize his strengths and resume such ordinary life activities as teaching, lecturing, and writing.

So, this morning I'm very frankly going to be speaking to you about people whom I think of as patients—or, at least as former or potential patients. Not only that—but I'll also be talking about patients who are chronically mentally ill—and I know that the word "chronic" has pejorative connotations for some people, too. But all I mean by it is that I'm going to be centering my remarks on people who have severe and persistent mental disorders that suggest that they may be dependent on mental health and supportive services for a very long time—sometimes for life.

My second digression, as I said, is going to take somewhat longer to complete, but I feel that I should pursue it before I turn my attention to the problems of research with young adult chronic patients and the homeless mentally ill. This digression concerns why I've even elected to talk to you about conceptual issues in a conference that's devoted to asking hard research questions. Am I being too philosophical? Am I being too picky?

I can assure you that I'm not. The issues that I want to discuss are absolutely critical to the conduct of effective research. They're at the very heart of what services for the chronically mentally ill in the 1980's are all about. And they're closely related to the games that we play in our field.

And we do indeed play games—games of denial, blame, and buck-passing—that ultimately affect patient care (Bachrach, 1985). And that, in a nutshell, is where our concern should be. We could live forever with fuzzy concepts, inadequate research designs, and irrelevant research results if they did not backfire to create problems in patient care. But, unfortunately, it's the people who are chronically mentally ill who ultimately end up paying for our ineptitude.

Now, we have a great many conceptual and related methodological problems that interfere in the conduct of relevant research in our field. Many of these problems are so general in the mental health field that you can't really think of them as the exclusive problems of researchers; they're shared by service planners and service providers. Other problems that we have in research are more or less specific to the research community—methodological problems that service providers typically don't think about—although maybe it wouldn't be such a bad idea if they did.

What often happens is that these two kinds of problems—the general conceptual ones that plague our field, and the more specifically methodological ones—combine subtly in such a way as to create serious impediments to the precise and controlled study of how to care for individuals who are chronically mentally ill.

A number of these problems seem to spring initially from our failure to define terms with anything that resembles precision. Researchers, planners, and service providers alike: we in mental health have historically had a discouraging habit of not explaining our terms. So, as a result, your guess is as good as mine, when it comes to understanding what our colleagues are talking about when they mention such basic terms as deinstitutionalization, community, least restrictive alternative, and the like. There's been a lack of consensus for these terms—and for many others—that's led to misunderstanding, confusion, and confounding of program efforts—to say nothing of research (Bachrach, 1985).

So we have this epidemic of chronic progressive fuzziness in our field. And, as if that's not enough, the condition is often masked. We're often unaware that this condition even exists—and so we compound our basic vagueness with ever more vagueness—and we don't even know that this interferes with the work we're trying to do.

Am I overstating the problem? I'll give you an example and let you be the judge. There's a growing body of research today that has to do with the effects of community support systems and community support interventions for the chronically mentally ill. But what, exactly, is a community support system? Does my community support system research talk about the same things as your community support system research? What does it all mean? What's a community? What's a support? And what's a system, anyway?

Now, as a matter of fact, when the National Institute of Mental Health (NIMH) mounted its Community Support Program (CSP) effort seven or eight years ago, it anticipated the semantic confusion that might arise in the use of the term community support system. And it made an effort to define the components of a community support system in order to mitigate this. That NIMH conceptualization is probably the most widely used understanding of community support systems in the field today, and I think that most of us are probably familiar with it. But I'd like to take just a minute anyway to review it.

According to the NIMH conceptualization, a community support system consists of ten essential components (Turner and Shifren, 1979), and I want to run through them:

First, the system has a mechanism for identifying the target population of chronically mentally ill individuals within a given community, and for reaching out to that population and offering services to those who wish them.

Second, the system offers special assistance to chronic mental patients in applying for, and gaining access to, special benefits and entitlements.

Third, the system offers 24-hour crisis assistance in a place called the "least restrictive setting possible"—although the meaning of restrictiveness is not precisely defined.

Fourth, the system provides psychosocial rehabilitation services to the target population.

Fifth, services provided within the system have an indefinite duration and are potentially available to patients throughout their lives.

Sixth, the system provides for adequate medical and mental health care for chronically mentally ill patients.

Seventh, the system includes backup supports for the family and friends of the patient, and also for other community members, in order to minimize the strains that are imposed by the long-term care needs of chronically disabled individuals.

Eighth, the system engages and involves concerned community members in such a way as to maximize the contributions of natural helping networks, self-help groups, and voluntary organizations that exist in the community, so that they may assist in the care of the chronically mentally ill.

Ninth, the system operates so as to protect patients' rights and ensure that their civil liberties are not denied.

And, tenth, the system provides for the binding, integration, and coordination of all the services that any particular chronic mental patient needs—a function that's described and defined as "case management."

Now, NIMH needs to be commended for this detailed conceptualization. The CSP Program represents the first federal effort ever to target the chronically mentally ill population exclusively, and to outline their program needs. The ten components in this conceptualization are both comprehensive and detailed; and they give us a pretty good feeling for what a community support system looks like.

But let's ask another question. Does this conceptualization allow us to plan programs uniformly? Or to do research that will yield uniform and standardized results? The answer to these questions, unfortunately, is no. For all its attempt to lend precision, the CSP conceptualization lacks the specificity of an operational definition. As it stands, it can't be used to identify and locate existing community support systems throughout the

United States. Nor can it be used as the basis for constructing new community support systems that are uniform enough to yield valid cross-study research results.

For starters, there's too much ambiguity in many of the terms. Any of us can get a pretty good argument going if we insist that we know *the* right way to define such terms as "least restrictive setting," "case management," "psychosocial rehabilitation," or "natural helping networks."

But that's only a small part of what's wrong. There's much worse. And to illustrate what I'm talking about, I'd like to pose a few questions for you:

What standard should we use to determine whether a community's services for the chronically mentally ill constitute a true community support system? How much of each of the ten components is needed in order for a particular effort to qualify? Do all ten criteria need to be present, or only some of them? And in what mix?

We even have problems with the first criterion all by itself—serious problems. How many and which chronically mentally ill people need to be reached, in order for a constellation of programs to qualify as a community support system? Do all chronically mentally ill people within a defined geographic area need to be reached? Can you have a community support system if you serve only some? And if you serve only some of them, how will you assign priorities within the population?

These are only a few of the many questions about community support systems that are, by and large, ignored in the NIMH conceptualization—and in the existing corpus of research. To me, this is an unfortunate circumstance, because it represents a golden opportunity that was lost—an opportunity to define populations, interventions, and outcomes at the inception of a widescale programmatic effort—and to define them with rigor and purpose. And, given current political realities, I don't know when we'll have another such opportunity.

Now, I don't mean to single out community support systems as the big villain. I've been talking about them only for illustrative purposes. The truth is that, in mental health research, we have many similar problems. We generally seem to have tremendous trouble in asking the right questions, in asking those questions in the right ways, and in placing those questions in cultural context—and part of the reason for this comes from semantic confusion.

If you're skeptical about the accuracy of what I'm saying, then consider these points:

If you want to measure outcomes of programs for chronic mental patients, how will you disentangle the many variables that contribute to an outcome (Bachrach, 1982a)? How will you distinguish the effects of medications versus the effects of psychotherapy, or psychosocial rehabilitation, or community support interventions, when all of them have been conducted simultaneously? Or even when they've been conducted serially?

Another group of questions concerns relapse. How much of relapse results from the illness itself, and how much comes from the inadequacy of treatment interventions? Does a readmission to inpatient care necessarily mean that the patient has relapsed? Or could a readmission simply mean that he or she lacks adequate community supports? How can you tell the difference?

And related to this: How should we view hospitalization? Does hospitalization necessarily mean treatment failure? A lot of the research we do makes that assumption. But isn't it possible that hospitalization sometimes simply means, "This is how the illness goes, and there are times when inpatient care will be necessary even under the best of circumstances"?

And, of course, these kinds of questions suggest a whole other problem that revolves around what service utilization patterns signify. Our research is often based on the assumption that the quality of patient care is reflected in utilization statistics—in the number of hospital admissions, or readmissions, or lengths of stay for people who are chronically mentally ill. But what justification do we have for these kinds of interpretations?

Now, at this point—having completed this rather long digression in order to provide you with some context—I'm prepared to become a little bit more specific. To go back to my opening story about polygamy in Israel: that confusion arose despite the existence of highly dedicated and well-trained researchers. It seems that they simply didn't know what they didn't know about their universe. We have many similar situations in the conduct of research on the chronically mentally ill.

And that brings me directly to the subject of the homeless mentally ill.

Today, there's a rapidly expanding literature on the population—a literature that ranges from thoughtful attempts to understand the problems of people who are homeless and chronically mentally ill, to special interest pieces that reflect the specific concerns of certain governmental, religious, or social service agencies.

But the bulk of this literature—whether it supports or indicts the homeless mentally ill—is pretty much in agreement on one very major point: That it's very hard to pinpoint the homeless mentally ill population (Bachrach, 1984b). A whole variety of factors seem to limit our efforts to define, to count, and to classify that population with any degree of precision.

I would say that there are at least five major problem areas that we need to deal with, when we try to define—and ultimately to count and classify and plan services for—people who are homeless and mentally ill. I want to look at each of these issues in a little bit of detail, because I think that they're very important. They're important not only with specific reference to the homeless mentally ill; but, beyond this, they're illustrative of some broad kinds of conceptual and methodological problems that we typically encounter in our field.

I think that a first major deterrent to defining and counting the homeless mentally ill population lies in our uncertainty about the precise meaning of homelessness *per se*. It's pretty widely agreed that homelessness implies both a lack of shelter and a dimension of disaffiliation, or social isolation. But this raises some questions:

What is shelter? And what is disaffiliation?

For example, is an automobile shelter? What about a cardboard box? Could a cardboard box maybe qualify as shelter in southern California, where it doesn't get too cold?

What about migrant farmworkers? Are they homeless? A lot of them actually live in shacks or huts—but most of us wouldn't really consider those places homes. But does our judgment of their residences qualify them as homeless?

And what about the Kickapoo Indians ("Lost" Indian Tribe, 1981)? This is a tribe of Indians who live under a bridge across the Rio Grande at Eagle Pass, Texas. They don't have much in the way of homes; at best they have some temporary reed huts. But they *do* have a tribal affiliation. They live together. Are they homeless?

I think you get the idea. Homlessness is hard to define.

But, as if that's not enough, we have some other kinds of problems superimposed on that when we try to define the homeless mentally ill. And these are problems that relate to confirming the presence of psychopathology among people who are homeless. (These are over and above the problems that we already have when we try to define chronic mental illness in general, which are complicated enough. I'm not even going to get into that one!)

Homeless people are often shy and frightened. It can take months just to approach some of them (Bachrach, 1984d). They often abuse alcohol and other drugs. And they're likely to have a subculture that encompasses entirely different values, norms, and behaviors from those of most mental health workers or researchers. All of these circumstances make differential diagnosis very difficult.

The fact that homeless people are also usually physically debilitated doesn't help the definitional problem either. Some investigators have been concerned over the validity of psychiatric diagnoses that are made on people whose basic subsistence needs are unmet. Two researchers who are pioneers in analyzing the needs are unmet. Two researchers who are pioneers in analyzing the needs of homeless mentally ill people—Baxter and Hopper (1982) in New York City—write quite persuasively that, "Were the same individuals to receive several nights of sleep, an adequate diet, and warm social contact, some of their symptoms might subside" (p. 402).

The combination of these two problem areas—difficulties in defining homelessness and difficulties in establishing the presence of psychopathology in a homeless population—this combination makes it easy for us to play a lot of number games with the homeless mentally ill. Even the federal government—or maybe I should say *especially* the federal government—has trouble estimating the size of the population.

To illustrate this:

For several years now, ADAMHA (the Alcohol, Drug Abuse and Mental Health Administration, 1983) has estimated that we have about two million homeless people in the United States—with about half of that number (that is, about one million people) suffering from alcohol, drug abuse, or mental health problems. But a more recent and significantly smaller estimate was released a year ago by the Department of Housing and Urban Development (HUD)—and it reduced the ADAMHA estimate by about 85 percent (U.S. Department of Housing and Urban Development, 1984). The HUD estimate says that there are only 250,000 to 300,000 homeless people in the United States—not two million.

I should point out, too, that this HUD estimate has been seriously—and I think very responsibly—challenged in Senate hearings (U.S. Senate, 1984). But HUD refuses to amend it, and the administration endorses it. You have to conclude that denial is a pretty good way to get rid of a problem that you don't want to face—the problem of providing care for a large homeless population.

A third problem that we have that's related to defining and counting homeless mentally ill people is the *overlap* of this population with other populations. The characteristics of the homeless mentally ill as a group can't be easily or readily distinguished from the characteristics of other groups of chronically mentally ill people that are discussed in the literature—groups like "revolving door" patients, or "treatment resistant" patients, or even "young adult chronic" patients (whom I'll be discussing in just a moment). There's a whole lot of blurring among all of these categories.

In fact, there was a study recently done at San Francisco General Hospital that identifies a subgroup of chronic mental patients who actually fit *all* of these labels (Goldfinger et al., 1984). These particular patients are frequent and regular users of inpatient and emergency psychiatric services at the San Francisco General Hospital—and also of outpatient, residential, and day treatment services in the community. Many of them are also intermittently homeless. In another study of the same population, Chafetz and Goldfinger (1984) have actually found that 46 percent of the admissions to psychiatric emergency services at San Francisco General Hospital are, or at some recent time have been, without stable housing.

I find this datum—this fact—very interesting. I think it tells us rather graphically that the boundary between the domiciled and the undomiciled chronically mentally ill populations is a very permeable one—and that these are probably not two separate populations. Instead, it's likely that they constitute one large population with some rather loose and shifting components.

The homeless mentally ill population is also, incidentally, sometimes hard to distinguish from certain populations in jails and correctional facilities. Lamb and Grant (1982, 1983) in California have reported that 36 percent of male, and 42 percent of female, inmates in Los Angeles County jail facilities, who were referred for psychiatric evaluation, had been living as transients on the streets, on the beaches, or in shelters at the time of their arrests.

So, then, we have problems in defining homelessness and in establishing the presence of psychopathology among homeless people. And we also have problems because of the overlap of this population with other populations.

A fourth kind of problem that we run into when we want to define and count the homeless mentally ill is the extreme diversity that exists *within* that population. This is a blindman-and-elephant kind of a methodological problem. We're apt to view the homeless mentally ill population in very parochial ways. But, like chronically mentally ill people in general, homeless mentally ill people aren't uniform—either diagnostically, demographically, or in terms of their residential or treatment histories.

On the basis of studies that they've done in Philadelphia, Arce (1983) and his colleagues (Arce et al., 1983) have divided the homeless mentally ill population into two major groupings. First, there are chronically homeless street people. Then there are the intermittently or episodically homeless people, who alternate between being domiciled and undomiciled. The episodically homeless tend to be younger than the chronically homeless, and they tend to have sporadic contacts with a variety of mental health and other community services. They tend to present as what's popularly called "difficult patients."

(Incidentally, Arce and his colleagues also describe a third category of homeless people—the situationally homeless, who are defined by situational stress (like unemployment, or spouse abuse), instead of by their psychopathology. For the situationally homeless, the absence of shelter is usually temporary, and the disaffiliation is less pronounced.)

The homeless mentally ill don't even constitute a uniform group in terms of their appearance. In New York City there's an outreach program called Project HELP (1983). Its mandate is to serve the most severely disabled among the homeless mentally ill. And this is how it describes its target population in an official report:

> The primary visual indicators include: extremely dirty and dishevelled appearance; obvious lice infestation; torn, dirty and/or layered clothing; weather inappropriate clothing (especially heavy coats and woolen hats in mid-summer); and a cache of belongings in bags, boxes, shopping carts, etc. The primary behavioral indicators include: walking in traffic, urinating and/or defecating in public, remaining mute and withdrawn (p. 4).

Now, this is a familiar kind of description: we've all seen these people, haven't we? But it can be contrasted with another description, by Reich and Siegel (1978) of a different group of mentally ill street people—also in New York City—who live on the Bowery. This is what Reich and Siegel have to say:

> Most of these men are intelligent and have better than the usual education found on the Bowery. They present a fairly intact appearance even when undergoing severe inner disturbance and thus can avoid unwanted hospitalization even when their situation destabilizes and there is a threat of erupting violence (pp. 195-196).

So, in other words, we can say that defining and counting the homeless mentally ill population is made very difficult by the fact that we have problems in extracting the common characteristics of such a heterogeneous population.

Last—but certainly not least—it's hard to define and count the homeless mentally ill because they vary so much geographically. Although they're often associated with inner-city residence, homeless mentally ill people are also found in small cities and in suburban and rural areas. Even *within* cities—as I've just indicated—there can be distinctive concentrations or clusters of homeless mentally ill people (Bachrach 1984d).

But not only do homeless mentally ill people differ according to where they are; they also vary according to how long they've been there. Some of them comprise an essentially stationary population that's relatively fixed within defined geographic limits—sometimes as small as a few city blocks. But others are very mobile over fairly large areas.

Several years ago, the Travelers Aid Society began to notice an upsurge of clients in what they referred to as "psychological flight"—and that this increase was occurring throughout the country. So in 1976 Travelers Aid did a study of people using their services in New Orleans. They found that 55 percent of the New Orleans clients who were judged by their workers to have severe and overt psychopathology were also picked up at Travelers Aid facilities in at least one other city—in addition to New Orleans. Moreover, 45 percent were seen in at least three other cities. And as many as 22 percent were seen in at least six other cities—in addition to New Orleans (Travelers Aid, 1976).

I think those are striking statistics. And I recently spoke with an official at the national headquarters of the Travelers Aid Society who told me that, if anything, the situation is still very much this way—if not more so.

Actually, migrating homeless mentally ill people are very widely reported in the literature. They've been documented in places like Arizona (Brown et al., 1983), California (Farr, 1982), Virginia (Chmiel et al., 1979), and Hawaii (Streltzer, 1979)—and even the Virgin Islands. I think that the common finding in all of these reports is summed up very neatly in a single sentence in an article by Streltzer who's written about mentally ill transients coming into Hawaii. Streltzer says, "Those who were attempting to escape psychosis continue to be psychotic in Hawaii" (p. 468).

I guess that I'd summarize this part of my talk on the homeless mentally ill by saying to you that we have a host of problems associated with defining, counting, and classifying the homeless mentally ill population—and these problems are quite serious. I think you can compare research with this population to a giant jigsaw puzzle. Every once in a while, we find a little piece of the puzzle. And when we're really lucky, we can lock two or three pieces together.

But the bottom line is that we don't have the perimeter of that puzzle. We don't really know what the outline of the whole thing—the universe—looks like. And the implications of that for research are obvious. How can we sample—in any sense of the word—or generalize, when we don't even know the parameters of the beast that we're dealing with? (Bachrach, 1984c).

But, if you look at the published research on the homeless mentally ill, you see that what's widely—and glaringly—missing from these reports is simple humility. With only a few exceptions, individual studies conducted on local subgroups of homeless mentally ill people more often than not generalize unabashedly about the universe.

Now, you're undoubtedly aware—even if you're just a little bit up on the current literature—that, in addition to the homeless mentally ill, there's another subgroup of the chronically mentally ill population that's getting a lot of press these days—and that's the population of young adult chronic patients (Bachrach, 1982b; Pepper et al., 1981).

Ever since the concept of the young adult chronic patient was introduced into the literature a few years ago, it's been rejected by some researchers and clinicians. It's been a controversial concept from the start. On a personal note, I find that my reaction to the concept has evolved from one of acceptance to one of concern. I've recently come to the conclusion that, in the future, I'm going to have to use the concept sparingly, for reasons that I hope to make clear.

According to the literature, young adult chronic patients exhibit some very special—and very troublesome—service needs. If I were to select some adjectives that are most often used to describe these patients in the literature, I'd probably choose words like "seriously ill," "frustrating," and "demanding."

These patients are frequently, but not exclusively, diagnosed with schizophrenic disorders—although diagnoses of affective disorders and, in some places, a borderline personality, are also quite prevalent. Substance abuse is often a contributing factor in their clinical course. In fact, the exposure to street drugs is widely considered to have severe biochemical consequences for these patients, and to influence the course of their pathology very critically.

In addition to this, many young adult chronic patients are reported to be geographically mobile—both within communities and between communities. Many of them move around a lot.

They also tend to be pervasive users of the mental health service system, and they utilize the entire range of facilities—so that we find them in state mental hospitals, in general hospitals, in community mental health centers, in private psychiatric hospitals, and in all kinds of outpatient psychiatric facilities.

However, at any given time, a substantial portion of the population of young adult chronic patients is reported to be *not* enrolled in mental health facilities and is essentially unserved by the mental health service system.

Those young adult chronic patients who do utilize their service system tend to do so in a revolving door manner and to move often from one facility to another. They also often use the criminal justice system in addition to, or else in place of, the mental health service system.

In many communities they become general hospital emergency room regulars. But their referral out of the emergency room to other facilities tends to be exceedingly problematic, because these patients are difficult to engage in treatment, and they appear to have no established niche within the mental health service system.

The vast majority of these young adult chronic patients are said to show very active patterns of service demand. They typically insist upon receiving, but they regularly and vociferously reject, a wide variety of service interventions.

Now, so much for a description of the population. Where did they all come from?

There seem to be two major reasons for their prominence in the population in the 1980s. In part, these patients represent the group of individuals who probably would have been institutionalized 25 or 30 years ao. And once admitted to institutions, they probably would have stayed there indefinitely. But today these patients have assumed increasing visibility in the mental health service system, very much as the result of deinstitutionalization policies and practices. They're no longer confined to institutions for life—and a sizable number of them never even enter institutions at all.

But I'm not implying that these young adult chronic patients are entirely an artifact of deinstitutionalization, because that's only part of the story. There's a second reason, too, for their emergence—and that has to do with the nation's changing demography.

These patients are drawn from the post-war baby-boom generation. And their numbers have been accumulating, as successive cohorts of post-war baby boom babies have been reaching the primary ages for onset of chronic mental illnesses. In other words, these patients are having an impact on the service system in absolute numbers—because there are just a lot of them around. And they're no longer hidden in institutions.

I think that it's fair to summarize the literature on these young adult chronic patients by saying that, generally speaking, they're largely out of place in today's service system—a service system that puts a lot of emphasis on the care of patients who are being discharged from state mental hospitals. As I just said, the fact is that many of these young patients never even enter state hospitals. And even those who do go into state hospitals tend to say for only a short while—maybe a few days or a few weeks—and then they're out in the community again.

What this means is that, in general, these patients are often circumstantially different from the state hospital resident patients of past years. Today's young adult chronic patients often live together. They sometimes travel together. And sometimes they reinforce one anothers' psychopathology. And, what's more, reports are now beginning to surface that these young adult chronic patients are experiencing some substantial fertility rates.

We're finally beginning to understand now that so-called "aftercare" programs often don't have a lot to offer young adult chronic patients—not because there's anything intrinsically wrong with aftercare; there isn't—but because those kinds of programs are generally directed toward the service needs of long-stay state hospital patients. At the same time, we're not exactly sure what kinds of programs young adult chronic patients *do* need. We're still in the process of learning, as H. Richard Lamb (1982) has so eloquently written. And these patients often throw us into confusion, and a lot of frustration, while we try to figure out what to do with them and for them.

In summary, what the concept of the young adult chronic patient tells us is that there's a group of chronically mentally ill people out there for whom the mental health service system, as it's now designed, is largely inadequate. This is the generation of patients who were supposed to have been beneficiaries of deinstitutionalization policies and practices. And now, as it were, they've "hit the streets"—both literally and figuratively—and they're testing those policies and practices—and often finding them wanting.

And, what's more, it's a very *large* generation of chronic mental patients numerically—because it draws from a base population that's been swelled by disproportionate birth rates. And the very size of the population is contributing to the problems we're encountering in trying to serve them.

Now, by focusing our attention on these young adult chronic patients, we've been able to sort out some of the very serious deficits in our service system, and that's been very appropriate for planning purposes. But, on closer examination, we're beginning to notice that the concept of the young adult chronic patient is full of conceptual and methodological flaws (Bachrach, 1984a). And, even though it's been valuable to us for planning purposes, it's showing itself to be a troublesome concept for research purposes. What's more, we're even beginning to wonder about its continued utility for planning purposes. True, it enhances our understanding of some problems; but it also distorts.

Many of the problems that I discussed in connection with research on the homeless mentally ill also confound research with young adult chronic patients. For example, their geographic mobility gives us problems. And, beyond this, we have difficulties when we try to establish the presence of psychopathology within a highly mobile and essentially non-treatment-oriented population. If people don't present for treatment—or if they won't stay at a treatment site long enough to be assessed and followed—then how can we ascertain the seriousness of their impairments?

But the most difficult conceptual problem with young adult chronic patients comes from our singling out a group of individuals *on the basis of their age*—and, in effect, saying that they're different from people of other ages who are chronically mentally ill: as if age is somehow a major independent variable.

Many clinicians have been turned off by this assumption. And they've rejected the concept of the young adult chronic patient on the basis that, from a clinical perspective, these patients are no different from older patients. They may be circumstantially different; but they still have the same kinds of illnesses and the same kinds of onsets. If they differ from older patients at all, it's only in their interactions with the service system. And there's nothing about their being young that distinguishes them.

This deserves some scrutiny. And, on closer examination, we find that it really is *not* their age as such that renders these young adults different from other chronic mental patients. Instead, it's the unique circumstances that surround their care. They're the first generation of chronic mental patients who have not been placed in structured long-term treatment settings—with all that implies: mobility, freedom, and access to street drugs.

You can even say that, as the first generation of patients to be served in an essentially deinstitutionalized service system, young adult chronic patients are often misfits within that system. They illustrate a cultural lag—to the extent that their special service needs were not foreseen and not accommodated.

Let me be just a little bit more specific about this. The young adult chronic patient population that was originally described in the literature was time-limited. When Pepper and his colleagues (1981) wrote their excellent article pointing up their characteristics and their service deficits, these patients were aged 18 to 35.

But that was four years ago—and that particular population today is between the ages of 23 and 39—and growing older by the minute. And a simple look at our demography tells us that we're very soon going to have a bulge of middle-aged chronic mental patients, and, then—not too long after that—a bulge of geriatric patients.

So what's our rationale for continuing to focus on 18-to-35-year-olds as if they constitute our major service problem? Those ages no longer describe the first post-deinstitutionalization generation of chronic mental patients. And if we perseverate in looking at 18-to-35-year-olds as our major planning challenge, we're going to miss the boat.

I would suggest to you that we need to think seriously about the validity of the concept of the young adult chronic patient. Maybe we need to use a different concept, so that we don't get confused by spurious age limits. And this is precisely what the British have done. In Great Britain, you don't hear about young adult chronic patients; you hear instead about "new long-term" patients (Shepherd, 1984; Wing and Morris, 1981). It's the same patient population, but it's called something else.

Now, maybe you remember that, in the past, the British have differentiated three kinds of chronic mental patients: old long-stay, new long-stay, and short-stay patients—designations that depend on when individuals entered institutions and on how long they stayed there (Bachrach, 1978). Now, by adding this new category—the new long-term patients—the British have acknowledged that we need a new designation for chronic mental patients today, because they can't be described by their institutional tenure any more. Some of them won't enter institutions at all.

And, what's more, the British concept isn't age-bound.

So, you see: By the simple expedient of focusing on patients' chronicity—on how disabled they are and how long they're likely to need care—and *not* focusing on their age, the British have avoided a problem that we're just beginning to understand—a problem that has to do with the fact that times change, and circumstances change. It's a conceptual issue of the first order, and one that has a profound impact on the research that we do.

So much for young adult chronic patients. My time is running out, and I now must try to make some concluding comments.

What I've done this morning is focus on two areas of inquiry—the homeless mentally ill and young adult chronic patients—in the hope of demonstrating to you how important it is, in the conduct of research on chronic mental patients, to ask the right questions in the right ways and with a sensitivity to cultural relevance. The conceptual and methodological problems that we run into with these two subpopulations symbolize more general problems we have in research. And with these two subpopulations—as in the rest of the field—we need to deal with a number of questions that precede the research questions, if we're going to design and conduct valid and reliable studies. There was nothing wrong with the question, "Are you happy with your wife?" technically. It was just the wrong question for that population.

Some of our research problems are strictly methodological ones. They're problems that we have to live with and deal with the best way that we can. For example, there's not much that we as researchers can do that will make it easier to ascertain the presence of psychopathology in a street person who's physically ill, frightened, and too wary to be approached.

But many of our research problems are conceptual, and they spring from semantic issues and fuzziness—and these things we *can* do something about.

If I had the time, I'd really like to talk to you about the reasons that we've gotten ourselves into this situation in our field—about what these conceptual problems really mean on a deeper level. I think that they're often symbolic of much wider-ranging issues than just research (Bachrach, 1985). They have to do with matters like stigma, denial, bandwagons, and our need to slow down if we're going to maintain any kind of equilibrium in our service system.

But I'm going to save that discussion for another conference.

The primary message I want to leave with you this morning is this: I believe that, as researchers, we have an obligation to clean up our act and to be advocates for clarity. There's an aphorism that I'm sure you've all heard: "Garbage in, garbage out." If we care about the research that we do—and, more importantly, if we care about the patients that the research is supposed to serve—then we need to take steps to eliminate the fuzziness in our thinking. We need to define our concepts with great care, and to pay attention to the subtleties that give us such serious research headaches.

Think of it this way: If we, as researchers, don't advocate for clarity and logic in our field, then who will?

Thank you.

REFERENCES

Alcohol, Drug Abuse and Mental Health Administration. (1983). *Alcohol, Drug Abuse and Mental Health Problems of the Homeless.* Rockville, MD: Alcohol, Drug Abuse and Mental Health Administration.

Arce, A. (1983). Statement Before the U.S. Senate Committee on Appropriations, Special Hearing on Street People. Washington: Government Printing Office.

Arce, A. (1983). Tadlock, M., Vergare, M. et al. (1983). A psychiatric profile of street people admitted to an emergency shelter. *Hospital and Community Psychiatry, 34,* 812-817.

Bachrach, L. (1978). A conceptual approach to deinstitutionalization. *Hospital and Community Psychiatry, 29,* 573-578.

Bachrach, L. (1982a). Assessment of outcomes in community support systems: Results, problems, and limitations. *Schizophrenia Bulletin, 8,* 39-61.

Bachrach, L. (1982b). Young adult chronic patients: An analytical review of the literature. *Hospital and Community Psychiatry, 33,* 189-197.

Bachrach, L. (1984a). The concept of young adult chronic psychiatric patients: questions from a research perspective. *Hospital and Community Psychiatry, 35,* 573-580.

Bachrach, L. (1984b). The homeless mentally ill and mental health services: An analytical review of the literature. In H. Lamb (Ed.), *The homeless mentally ill.* Washington: American Psychiatric Association.

Bachrach, L. (1984c). Interpreting research on the homeless mentally ill: Some caveats. *Hospital and Community Psychiatry, 35,* 914-917.

Bachrach, L. (1984d). Research on services for the homeless mentally ill. *Hospital and Community Psychiatry, 35,* 910-913.

Bachrach, L. (1985). *Slogans and euphemisms: The functions of semantics in mental health and mental retardation care.* Austin, TX: Hogg Foundation.

Baxter, E. & Hopper, K. (1982). The new mendicancy: Homeless in New York City. *American Journal of Orthopsychiatry, 52,* 393-408.

Brown, C., MacFarlane, S., Paredes, R. et al. (1983). *The homeless of Phoenix: Who are they? And what should be done?* Phoenix South Community Mental Health Center.

Chafetz, L. & Goldfinger, S. (1984). Residential instability in a psychiatric emergency setting. *Psychiatric Quarterly, 56,* 20-34.

Chmiel, A., Akhtar, S., & Morris, J. (1979). The long-distance psychiatric patient in the emergency room. *International Journal of Social Psychiatry, 25,* 38-46.

Ehrenreich, J. (1982). Where the health dollar really goes. *The Nation,* 15 May 1982, 586-588.

Farr, R. (1982). Skid row project. Los Angeles County Department of Mental Health, Jan. 18, 1982.

Goldfinger, S., Hopkin, J., & Surber, R. (1984). Treatment resisters or system resisters? Toward a better service system for acute care recidivists. *New Directions for Mental Health Services, 21,* 17-27.

Ingelfinger, F. (1984). Arrogance. *New England Journal of Medicine, 303,* 1507-1511.

Lamb, H. (1982). Young adult chronic patients: The new drifters. *Hospital and Community Psychiatry, 33,* 465-468.

Lamb, H. & Grant, R. (1982). The mentally ill in an urban county jail. *Archives of General Psychiatry, 39,* 17-22.

Lamb, H. & Grant, R. (1983). Mentally ill women in a county jail. *Archives of General Psychiatry, 40,* 363-368.

"Lost" Indian tribe seeks recognition and a home. *New York Times,* 26 December 1982, 12.

Pepper, B., Kirshner, M., & Ryglewicz, H. (1981). The young adult chronic patient: Overview of a population. *Hospital and Community Psychiatry, 32,* 463-469.

Project HELP Summary, 30 October 1982–31 August 1983. New York State Community Support Services, Gouverneur Hospital, New York City, 1983.

Reich, R. & Siegel, L. (1978). The emergence of the Bowery as a psychiatric dumping ground. *Psychiatric Quarterly, 50,* 191-201.

Shepherd, G. (1984). *Institutional care and rehabilitation.* London: Longman.

Streltzer, J. (1979). Psychiatric emergencies in travelers to Hawaii. *Comprehensive Psychiatry, 20,* 463, 468.

Talbott, J. (1984). Viewpoint. *Psychiatric News,* 20 July 1984, 2, 14.

Travelers Aid Society of Greater New Orleans. (1976). Summary of study of wandering mentally ill.

Turner, J. & Shifren, I. (1979). Community support systems: How comprehensive? *New Directions for Mental Health Services,* No. 2, 1-23.

U.S. Department of Housing and Urban Development. (1984). A report to the Secretary on the homeless and emergency shelters.

U.S. Senate. (1984). HUD report on homelessness. Washington: U.S. Government Printing Office.

Wing, J. & Morris, B. (1981). Clinical basis of rehabilitation. In J. Wing and B. Morris (Eds.), *Handbook of psychiatric rehabilitation practice.* Oxford: Oxford University Press.

Chapter 3

Families with a Chronically Mentally Ill Member: A Review of the Research Findings

LeRoy Spaniol and Anthony Zipple

The current trend in the treatment of the severely psychiatrically disabled emphasizes community-based approaches. This has resulted in short periods of hospitalization and use of a wide array of aftercare and rehabilitation services. Community-based treatment has also enabled large numbers of psychiatrically disabled persons to return to their families. Several studies have reported that 22 to 66 percent of deinstitutionalized patients return to their families (Goldman, 1982; Lamb & Oliphant, 1978; Minkoff, 1979). There are approximately 800,000 severely psychiatrically disabled people living in the community, and up to 500,000 of these are living at home (Goldman & Gatozzi, 1981). It is clear that families have become primary caregivers for the severely psychiatrically disabled.

Families have been viewed from different perspectives throughout the history of psychiatric treatment. Frequently, as Kreisman and Joy (1974) found in their comprehensive review of the literature, families were considered a major stressor and cause of schizophrenia, as in Fromm-Reichmann's (1948) concept of the "schizophrenogenic" mother. While this stigmatizing viewpoint has been discounted (Arieti, 1984), a variety of systems-oriented theories attribute mental illness to the family. In their conceptualizations, mental illness is seen as a manifestation of problems within the entire family, which is seen as a unit consisting of interacting parts and which operates under a set of rules that mutually determine the behavior of all family members (Bateson, Jackson, Haley, & Weakland, 1956; Bowen, 1960; Hirsch & Leff, 1975; Lidz, 1958; Wynne, Ryckoff, Day, & Hirsch, 1958). In a pure systems approach, no single individual is blamed for the illness of another family member, but all family members are seen as following implicitly defined rules that regulate the system in a homeostatic manner (Messer, 1970). Homeostasis is maintained even under circumstances involving pathology because the family is locked into this mode of functioning. Although family members are not explicitly blamed, they are implicitly held responsible. This model asserts that all members contribute to the pathological condition.

Recent work has considered the family as a "reactor." The person who is reacting is not causing psychiatric disability but is responding to the ill family member's behavior. Rather than blaming the family members or "benignly" attributing responsibility to them for one member's psychiatric condition, this viewpoint sees the family as responding to psychiatric disability through coping and adaptation (Hatfield, 1978, 1979; Jung, Spaniol, & Anthony, 1983; Kint 1978). This change in viewpoint allows a comprehensive and pragmatic approach to examining family-patient interaction and adaptation. A nonblaming stance broadens the possibilities for helping the family and considers the family's positive role in relation to psychiatric disability.

This new perspective on families of the mentally ill is receiving increased attention in the mental health research literature. This paper will summarize (a) the current research on the needs of families with mentally ill members and professional responses to these families; (b) the coping strategies employed by these families; and (c) innovative models for working with families of the mentally ill.

THE NEEDS OF FAMILIES OF THE MENTALLY ILL AND THE PERCEPTIONS OF MENTAL HEALTH PROFESSIONALS

A small but growing number of studies have attempted systematically to assess the needs of families by directly asking family members to report on what they need to be effective care givers for their disabled relative (Creer & Wing, 1974; Doll, 1976; Hatfield, 1978; Holden & Lewine, 1982; Spaniol, Jung, Zipple, & FitzGerald, 1984; Wasow, 1980). The samples used in most of these studies are drawn from existing self-help groups, such as chapters of the National Alliance for the Mentally Ill (NAMI). The membership of the National Alliance for the Mentally Ill is not representative of all families of the mentally ill—NAMI families are primarily middle- and upper-class, and few are from minority groups. Although this limits the generalizations that can be made from the findings, the aggregate results are still helpful in describing the needs of families with psychiatrically disabled relatives.

An even smaller number of surveys have attempted to assess family satisfaction with professional assistance (Hatfield, Fierstein, & Johnson, 1983; Holden & Lewine, 1982; Spaniol et al., 1984; Wasow, 1980). Results show that many professionals need to improve their skills, increase their knowledge, and change their attitudes about the needs of these families. A caveat about the limitations of research in this area should be stated. Most of the studies on family needs, satisfaction, and professional/family relationships are based on survey-research strategies, which are limited because they rely on the self-reports of respondents. Survey research cannot control the factors that influence the responses of study subjects and does not permit an objective assessment of family functioning. Nevertheless, survey research can be a powerful explanatory tool and can help suggest appropriate questions for controlled research.

In addition to the limitations of survey research, many studies, including the one described below, use self-reports of satisfaction as the central means of understanding how families cope with their chronically ill member. Measures of satisfaction are, by their nature, subjective, and do not necessarily correlate with more objective, assessments of family functioning or professional/family relationships.

Measures of satisfaction also depend on the context—the more satisfied one's life is at the time of the measure, the more likely that ratings of satisfaction will be high in general.

Jung, Spaniol, and Anthony (1983) have suggested that family needs reported in these studies (and by implication professional needs in providing assistance) can be divided into five major categories:

1. Information about mental illness;
2. Assistance in managing psychiatric symptoms;
3. Assistance in managing problematic behavior;
4. Assistance with psychiatric medications;
5. Assistance in coping with stress.

Each is discussed below.

Need For Information About Mental Illness

Families consistently express a need for information about the etiology, treatment, and progress of mental illness. Wasow (1980) found in her survey of 50 parents of adults with schizophrenic disorders that one of the seven most frequently reported need was for "better explanation of the illness." Families find good explanations helpful, but report a low level of satisfaction with the quantity and quality of information about mental illness provided by professionals. Spaniol et al. (1984) found in their national survey of NAMI members that 21.2 percent of the families surveyed reported their most important need was for information about the illness. However, 53.1 percent of the families reported that professionals had not helped them to understand their relative's disorder, and 26.3 percent reported being very dissatisfied with the level of information provided. This is a striking contrast with the survey by Spaniol et al. (1984) of mental health professionals, in which 69 percent of the professionals believed that families were generally satisfied with the information which was provided.

Most families want to know the psychiatric diagnosis of their disabled relative. Wasow (1980) found that only 17 percent of the families felt they had been given an accurate psychiatric diagnosis of their adult child's disorder within one year of seeking professional help. Another 17 percent waited from six to fifteen years before receiving a diagnosis. This figure is consistent with Holden and Lewine's (1982) survey, which found that 32 percent of the relatives were given a diagnosis only two to eleven years after the initial breakdown. Holden and Lewine also found that the diagnosis was vague and inadequately explained. Spaniol et al. (1984) also report similar results. Thirty-eight percent of the family members they surveyed were given a diagnosis only after one year or more; 58 percent found that professional assistance in understanding the illness was inadequate. Hatfield (1979) found in her survey of relatives of psychiatrically disabled adults that 57 percent of the respondents reported a need to better understand symptoms. This finding is consistent with Hatfield's later survey (1983) of families, in which 59 percent of the respondents listed "learning about the nature of mental illness" as a major therapy goal. On the other hand, only 24 percent of the therapists surveyed by Hatfield listed this as a major therapy goal. Hatfield (1978; 1979; 1983) concludes that families want and need more information about the psychiatric illness of their relatives and that mental health professionals are often unwilling or unable to provide it.

Mental health professionals often do not provide adequate levels of information about mental illness to families with psychiatrically disabled relatives, despite the families' wish to have such information. An explanation of this communication gap can be found in surveys which suggest that professionals are often unaware of family needs and of family dissatisfaction with the information being provided (Hatfield et al., 1983; Jung et al., 1983).

Need for Assistance in Managing Psychiatric Symptoms

A second major need expressed by families with psychiatrically disabled members is for assistance in managing the primary symptomatology of their disabled relative. The symptoms—hallucinations, delusions, paranoia, catatonia, mania, and inappropriate affect—are often very disturbing for families (Bernheim, Lewin, & Beale, 1982; Hatfield, 1978; Wasow, 1982).

Spaniol et al. (1984) found that symptom management was a significant problem for families and that 39 percent of the family members surveyed believed that symptoms could not be managed at home.

Families express a need for both information and skills that will be helpful in symptom management. Information about symptoms can be helpful to families (Anderson, Hogarty & Reiss, 1980). In addition, families want skills to help them with symptom management. Spaniol et al. (1984) found that "practical advice" was one of their three most important areas of need. Forty-one percent of the families on this survey reported that schizophrenic symptoms or depressions are the most troubling and burdensome behavior exhibited by their relative. However, 46 percent of the families were dissatisfied with the quality of practical advice offered by mental health professionals. Twenty percent of the families reported that advice was incomplete, while 12 percent felt that the advice was too vague. It should be noted that this high level of dissatisfaction occurs in spite of the finding of Spaniol et al. (1984) that 70 percent of mental health professionals believed that families were satisfied with the level of practical advice they provided.

Hatfield (1983) found that assistance in managing symptoms was a concern for most family members. Sixty-two percent of the family members surveyed reported that "learning to respond to psychiatric symptoms such as hearing voices, talking to self, and paranoia" was a goal of their therapy. However, 37.1 percent of the families surveyed reported receiving no help in this area from professionals. The large number of family members who report receiving no help may be explained by the fact that only 11 percent of the therapists surveyed reported that "learning to respond to symptoms" was a focus of therapy (Hatfield et al., 1983).

Holden and Lewine (1982) report findings that support the preceding studies. In their survey, only 9 percent of the family members responding report that "learning strategies for coping with symptomatic behavior" is their "primary response" to contact with mental health professionals. This contrasts with the 68 percent who report frustration, anger, powerlessness, or guilt as their primary response to contact.

Families want and need assistance in managing the psychiatric symptoms of their disabled family member. Mental health professionals have often been unwilling to provide families with practical advice on strategies for doing so. This may be explained by findings which suggest that many professionals are unaware of these needs and of family member dissatisfaction with professional efforts to help meet these needs.

Need for Assistance in Managing Problematic Behavior

In addition to overt symptoms, psychiatrically disabled individuals often display a variety of related behaviors that are disturbing and intrusive—unusual sleeping and eating patterns, aggression, self-destructiveness, deviant sexual behavior, poor self-care habits, and withdrawal (Bernheim, Lewine, & Beale, 1982; Torrey, 1983; Hyde, 1980; Spaniol et al., 1984; Wasow, 1982).

Spaniol et al. (1984) found that "practical advice" was reported as one of the three most important needs identified by families. Spaniol et al. also found that 47 percent of the families listed aggressiveness, withdrawal, self-injury, grooming and hygiene, household chores, sleeping patterns or listlessness, and low energy as the most burdensome and troubling behavior exhibited by the disabled relative. However, 46 percent of family members were dissatisfied with the quality of advice provided by professionals. Again, most professionals believed that families were generally satisfied with these services.

Hatfield et al. (1983) found that most families listed the management of specific problem behaviors as a goal for therapy. Eighty-nine percent listed "learning to motivate the patient to do more," 52 percent listed "learning how to handle threats of violence," 47 percent listed "getting better hygiene with patients," and 42 percent listed "helping control substance abuse." At the same time, 44.2 percent reported receiving no help in motivating the patient, 37.3 percent reported receiving no help in responding to threats of violence, 63.8 percent reported receiving no help with achieving better hygiene, and 45 percent reported receiving no help with patient substance abuse.

These figures may be explained by the fact that less than 18 percent of the therapists surveyed reported any of these topics as goals for therapy (Hatfield, 1983).

Families want and need assistance in managing the problem behaviors of their psychiatrically disabled family member, but they are dissatisfied with the assistance provided by mental health professionals. Again, professionals are often unaware of family needs and family dissatisfaction with their attempts at assistance.

Need for Assistance with Psychiatric Medications

Psychoactive medications are usually an important part of the overall treatment of most psychiatric disabilities (Hogarty, Goldberg, & Schooler, 1975; May, Tuma, & Dixon, 1976). Spaniol et al. (1984) and Holden and Lewine (1982) both found that 95 percent of the family members surveyed reported that their psychiatrically disabled relative was receiving medication. Family members often report a need for both information and skills that will assist them in helping their disabled relative to manage their medications.

Spaniol et al. (1984) found that "drug medication" was listed by 18 percent of the family respondents as their most important need. However, 92 percent were dissatisfied with the quality of medication services. Forty-seven percent reported not being informed about how medication would help, 60 percent reported not being informed about side effects, and 78 percent reported not being informed about long-term side effects.

Holden and Lewine (1982) reported similar findings. Only 53 percent of the family members surveyed reported receiving information on why medication was being prescribed. Only 24 percent received information about possible side effects of the medication services. These figures contrast sharply with the finding that 60 percent of mental health professionals believe that families are generally satisfied with medication services (Spaniol et al. 1984).

Hatfield (1983) also found that information and skills related to medication was an important need for families. Seventy-six percent of the families she surveyed reported that "understanding medications and their use" was a goal for therapy, 74 percent reported "learning potential side effects" as a goal, and 54 percent reported "achieving compliance with medication" as a goal. The percentage of therapists listing one of these three problems as a goal ranged from a high of 25 percent for "learning potential side effects of medication" to a low of 19 percent for "achieving compliance with medication." This may explain why the percentages of families who reported receiving no help with these goals ranged from 27.6 to 38.9 percent (Hatfield et al., 1983).

In summary, families want and need assistance in understanding and helping with the psychiatric medications used by their disabled family members. However, professionals are often unwilling or unable to provide this service. Most professionals surveyed were unaware of the families' need and their high level of dissatisfaction with medication services.

Need for Assistance in Coping with Stress

The task of caring for a psychiatrically disabled relative is demanding and may create serious stresses for other family members (Jung et al., 1983). More than 50 percent of family members surveyed by Spaniol et al. (1984) experienced a sense of burden, anxiety, frustration, and worry during the 12 months prior to the survey. More than 40 percent of those family members experienced an increased sense of depression, grief, fear, and anger. More than 25 percent experienced increased levels of physical problems, guilt, and sleep disturbances. In addition, families face serious financial strain in their effort to provide care; 42 percent of the family members in this survey reported that caring for their disabled family member had affected their family finances "much" or "very much."

Hatfield (1978) found that 65 percent of the families that she surveyed reported stress from caring for their disabled relative. The families also reported such other effects as disruption of the marriage, hardships for siblings, decreased social contacts and leisure time, resentment, grief, and depression. Hatfield concludes that "families of the mentally ill risk the deterioration of their psychological and physical resources to the point that their personal efficiency may be reduced and the organization and stability of their family life threatened" (p. 358).

A later study by Hatfield (1983) found that many families reported that reducing stress was a goal for therapy. Seventy percent reported that "reduction of anxiety about patient" is a major need in therapy, 44 percent listed "helping gain order and control over household," 37 percent listed "getting acceptance of patient by spouse," and 34 percent listed "gaining time for personal life." However, less than 25 percent of therapists surveyed listed any of these needs as a focus of therapy.

Holden and Lewine (1982) report similar findings. Seventy-eight percent of their respondents reported increased family tension since the onset of their relative's disability. Of those 78 percent (n = 187), 25 percent reported a major life disruption, such as divorce, that they believed to be related to the stress of a family member's disability. Forty-seven percent of those families also reported increased health problems. Seventy-four percent of the families report moderate-to-severe financial problems due to the cost of caring for their disabled relative.

Thompson and Doll (1982) surveyed 125 family members to assess both objective and subjective levels of burden imposed by caring for a psychiatrically disabled relative. Objective burden was defined as "disruptions which the former patient has on family life." Indicators included financial burden, role strains, disruptions of everyday routine, supervision time, and problems with neighbors. Forty-six percent of the family members reported one or two of these problems, and 27 percent reported three or more. Thompson and Doll concluded that 73 percent of the families experience moderate-to-severe levels of òbjective burden. Subjective burden was defined as "felt stresses" imposed by caring for their disabled relative. Indicators included feelings of embarrassment, overload, entrapment, resentment, and exclusion. Fifteen percent òf the families surveyed experienced at least two of these, and 62 percent of the families reported three or more. The authors conclude that 77 percent of the families experienced moderate-to-severe levels of subjective burden.

Quantitative studies of the degree to which mental health professionals are able to help families cope with these stresses are not available. However, the studies reviewed in the preceding pages clearly indicate that families are generally dissatisfied with mental health professionals, do not generally find them helpful, and often feel blamed by them for the disability of their mentally ill relative. From these results it may be inferred that many mental health professionals have been unable or unwilling to assist families in coping with stresses created by caring for a psychiatrically disabled relative. This failure to assist occurs in spite of the strong evidence that families want and need help from professionals in these areas.

Summary of Family Needs and Perceptions of Mental Health Professionals

Individuals who care for a psychiatrically disabled relative often have serious needs for skills, information, and support in the five preceding areas of concern. These needs have been expressed consistently in a small but significant number of surveys conducted between 1978 and 1984. Despite the intensity of these needs and the consistency with which they are reported, professionals are often unable or unwilling to respond effectively to meet those needs. In fact, there is evidence that many professionals who work with these families are unaware of their wants, needs, and perceptions of mental health services.

There is little systematic research on family response to assistance from mental health professionals that more closely matches their expressed needs for skill, information, and support in the five areas of need. It seems reasonable to assume that families would respond in a more positive fashion. In addition, there is strong anecdotal evidence that families find it helpful when professionals give them what they say they want and need (Bernheim et al., 1982; Park & Shapiro, 1976; Plummer, Thornton, Seeman, & Littman, 1984; Walsh, 1985; Willis, 1982). It can be inferred that the professional interventions that families find most helpful are those which respond to the families' perceived wants and needs. The following section reports on the few studies in which families were given the support, information, and/or skills that they seem to want and need.

INNOVATIVE APPROACHES TO ASSISTING FAMILIES

During the past five years, there has been increased interest in developing and evaluating interventions that meet the self-perceived needs of families with mentally ill members. The most important innovations in assistance to families has been in providing education and support (Beels & McFarlane, 1982). Such approaches are useful and important for two reasons. First, it appears that families with psychiatrically disabled relatives often prefer support and education to such traditional interventions as family therapy (Hatfield, 1979, 1981). Second, there is a growing body of evidence that these approaches result in significantly improved outcomes for the disabled family member (Anderson, Hogarty, & Reiss, 1981; Byalin, Jed, & Lehman, 1982; Falloon, Boyd, McGill et al., 1982).

While educational and supportive approaches are both useful to families and effective in reducing relapse rates, it may be difficult for the practitioner to decide which of the approaches would be the intervention of choice for a specific family. Existing educational and supportive models offer advantages as well as limitations.

Existing approaches can be divided into four general categories:

1. Educational approaches designed primarily to provide information
2. Skill-training approaches designed to develop skills
3. Supportive approaches designed to enhance the family's emotional capacity to cope with stress
4. Comprehensive approaches that incorporate information, skill training, and support in a single intervention.

Most models use elements of more than one of these approaches. However, these conceptual divisions are useful providing a clear image of the central goal of the intervention.

Information-Sharing Approaches

Information-sharing approaches are interventions designed to provide information about psychiatric disability and its management. The goal of information-sharing models is to increase the family members' understanding of their disabled relative's disorder and of the interventions that may be helpful in treating the disorder. Typically, family members learn about the etiology, symptoms, and the course of disabling psychiatric disorders. Additionally, they learn about various treatments, such as medications, psychotherapy, and psychosocial rehabilitation programs. While many information-sharing approaches offer practical advice about caring for a psychiatrically disabled relative, they do not generally teach specific skills to participants. That is they do not focus on skill demonstration, skill practice, feedback, or skill-based homework assignments.

One information-sharing approach currently being used was developed by Anderson, Hogarty, and their associate (Anderson, 1983; Anderson, Hogarty, & Reiss, 1980; 1981). The model has two goals: first, it attempts to decrease patient vulnerability to environmental stimulation through a program of maintenance chemotherapy; second, it attempts to increase the level of stability and predictability of the family environment by decreasing family members' anxiety about the patient, increasing their knowledge about the disorder, and increasing their confidence in their ability to be effective caregivers.

There are four parts to the intervention. First, the clinician establishes a relationship with the family. This process, which is referred to as "connecting," consists of eliciting the family's experience with its disabled relative, mobilizing family concern, establishing the clinician as the family's ombudsman, and developing a treatment contract.

The second phase of the process is a one-day, multi-family workshop referred to as a "survival skills workshop." It should be noted, however, that the primary goal of the day is to provide information rather than skill training. Information about the disorder and medications are always included. Additionally, practical advice about management of the disorder is provided. Finally, family members are encouraged to be concerned about their own lives and stress levels and are given permission to maintain a relatively normalized life style in spite of their family member's disability.

The third part consists of family sessions every two to three weeks for six months to a year, in which application of the information supplied during the one-day workshop is monitored. Special attention is paid to developing respect for interpersonal boundaries and enhancing the personal responsibility of the disabled family member.

The final part of the intervention is a decision to continue the family sessions, modify the arrangement, or terminate the intervention. There is no specific time limit on the length of the intervention. Most families spend at least two years in treatment (Anderson, 1983).

The results of this approach are encouraging. The rate of relapse of disabled individuals whose families participate in the model is less than 10 percent, compared to a relapse rate of 34 percent in the control group. This low relapse rate is achieved in spite of the fact that most patients continue to experience some severe levels of disability (Anderson, Hogarty, & Reiss, 1981).

A second information-sharing approach was developed by Dincin, Selleck, and Streiker (1978) at Thresholds, an established psychosocial rehabilitation center. The primary goal of the model is to restructure parental attitudes toward a psychiatrically disabled family member by providing them with information about the disorder and its management. Specifically, the program is designed to help parents allow and encourage separation from the parental home. During the time that family members are in the program (usually 12 weeks), they are given information about the etiology and management of the disorder and encouraged not to feel guilty or responsible. Instead, it is suggested that emancipation is best for both the family and the disabled person.

The results of the program are encouraging. Sixty percent of the parents who participated reported that the group helped them to make significant gains. In addition, significantly more disabled family members of participants left the parental home during the course of the group, as compared to the adult children of nonparticipants. This is important, for having the disabled family member in the home has been found to correlate with both decreased levels of satisfaction for the nondisabled family member (Spaniol et al., 1984) and an increased sense of burden (O'Conner, 1983).

A final example of an information-sharing approach is provided by Hatfield (1984). Hatfield's program entails six two-hour seminars that families attend weekly. Each week, a different subject is discussed. Topics include (1) the meaning of mental illness to the family, (2) understanding chronic mental illness, (3) the treatment for mental illness, (4) creating a low stress environment, (5) managing disturbing behavior, and (6) promoting growth and rehabilitation. The emphasis is on cognitive mastery of the material. Participants are encouraged to share relevant personal experiences and insights. The atmosphere is informal but task-oriented. A wide range of reading material, including the training manual, is utilized. While this model seems promising, no data on participant satisfaction or patient outcome is provided.

These three models, and other similar approaches, share three strengths. First, they provide specific information in each of the five major areas of need described in the previous section. Since these models provide some of what families seem to want, it is likely that families would experience the models as useful and satisfying. Second, all of the models emphasize teaching rather than treating families, which limits the possibility of families feeling blamed by professionals for their relatives' disorders and, in turn, enhances the willingness of families to participate in the intervention (Wasow, 1980). Additionally, there is less stigma attached to educational approaches than to therapy (Hatfield et al., 1983), which again enhances the willingness of families to participate. Third, in each of these models the professional functions as a consultant to the family and displays a willingness to share control over interventions with other family members. This willingness to include the family as a partner is both satisfying for families (Hatfield, 1979) and liberating for professionals, since they are able to utilize other family members as resources in caring for the disabled individuals (Spaniol, Zipple, & Fitzgerald, 1984).

Despite these strengths, all information-sharing approaches have similar limitations. Recent surveys of family needs suggest that families need both information and specific skills to be effective caregivers (Hatfield 1979; Spaniol et al., 1984; Wasow, 1980). While information-sharing programs seem to recognize the importance of both information and skills, they primarily provide information to participants. These information-based interventions can be effective. However, they may not be powerful enough if the family wants and needs skills as well. Many families may only want or need information. However, to produce maximum levels of satisfaction and effectiveness, some families may require more powerful or intensive assistance.

An additional limitation is the failure of current information-sharing models to include material on family advocacy. Advocacy is an important function of families, one that families have become more adept at and familiar with through the self-help movement. Advocacy is an important coping mechanism, and information about it should be included in educational approaches.

Skill-Training Approaches

Skill-training approaches are interventions that directly and systematically teach specific behaviors that will enhance care-giving abilities of families with a psychiatrically disabled member. The goal is to increase the family members' ability to be helpful to the disabled family member and manage that member's psychiatric disorder more effectively. Typically, individuals are taught a range of communication skills, problem-solving skills, limit-setting techniques, and such basic behavioral interventions as how to use rewards, develop contracts, and define problem behaviors. Most skill-training programs offer information to trainees, but the primary emphasis is on the acquisition and application of skills.

One of the most sophisticated skill-training approaches for

families with psychiatrically disabled relatives has been developed by the Mental Health Clinical Research Center for the Study of Schizophrenia (Falloon, Libermann, Little, & Vaughn, 1981; Liberman, Wallace, Vaughn, & Snyder, 1979). This group has developed and evaluated a ten-week series of two-hour training sessions for family members and their disabled relatives (Liberman, Aitchison, & Falloon, 1979). The goals of the program are to strengthen the problem-solving skills of the disabled family member and to improve the emotional climate in the home by training all family members in communication skills. The program draws heavily from the work on "expressed emotion" in the family (Brown, Birley, & Wing, 1972; Leff & Vaughn, 1980). This research suggests that relapse is related to the level of negative emotion towards the disabled individual by other family members, and that teaching relatives to moderate the expression of such emotions will lead to improved outcome.

The first two weeks of the program are informational discussions of the nature of schizophrenia and medications. The next five weeks teach a series of problem-solving and communication skills to family members. Skills such as listening, expressing positive and negative feelings, and aftercare planning are covered. The ninth week is a review and good-bye session. The tenth week, which occurs three months later, is a follow-up to the problem-solving skill session and an opportunity to collect outcome data. During this same period, all disabled relatives of the trainees receive similar problem-solving and communication skills in separate training meetings. Each skill-training session contains behavioral descriptions of the skill practice exercises and related homework assignments. The disabled individuals who participated in this program with their relatives had a significantly lower relapse rate at a 12-month follow-up than the control-group subjects, who received holistic interventions including insight-oriented family therapy. Follow-up studies using these and additional related methods also report positive results (Falloon, Boyd, & McGill, 1984).

Goldstein and Kopeikin (1981) report on the impact of a short-term treatment program combined with chemotherapy. While the program is described as "crisis-oriented therapy" (Kopeikin, Marshall, & Goldstein, 1983), the therapy appears to consist largely of skills training. The program is a series of six weekly family sessions following the discharge of the patient from a hospital setting. The model emphasizes the importance of stress management and has four specific goals: first, it helps the family members learn how to identify situations that are stressful for the patient; second, it attempts to teach strategies for avoiding or coping with stress; third, it teaches families to evaluate and refine their stress-management techniques; finally, the program teaches families to anticipate stressful situations and to plan proactive responses to them.

Results of this approach are encouraging. None of the 25 patients who participated in these sessions with their families and received relatively high doses of medication experienced a relapse during a six-month follow-up, compared to a 48 percent relapse rate for a control group receiving low doses of medication and no therapy. While the simultaneous manipulation of multiple variables makes precise interpretation of the results difficult, the authors conclude that a combination of medication and family education is effective in reducing relapse.

All of these skill-training approaches to helping families share similar strengths. First, each is designed to provide family members with specific behaviors that may be useful in their attempts to be effective care givers. For families who want and need an intervention more powerful than information alone, skill training may be the approach of choice. Second, each approach is potentially nonstigmatizing in that the professional's role is more like that of a teacher than of a traditional therapist. The less like therapy the intervention appears, the more likely that families will experience it as a helpful intervention (Hatfield, 1979; Wasow, 1980).

Skill-training approaches also share three significant limitations. First, each model assumes the importance of a set of skills and then attempts to teach families what it has to offer. The trainer comes to the session with a training curriculum and a belief that the families attending want and need to learn communication skills, problem-solving skills, stress-management skills, and so on. The skill-training approach is only as useful as this belief is valid. If some families do not want and need these skills, these approaches may be less helpful or satisfying to them. Second, there is an unnecessary tendency to describe some of these interventions as therapy or treatment rather than education or training (Falloon, Liberman, Lillie, & Vaughn, 1981; Kopeikin, Marshall, & Goldstein, 1983). This may be the result of insurance reimbursement pressures, professional status issues, or professional training models. Whatever the reasons, this tendency poses a risk. The more therapy-like the intervention appears to families, the more likely it is that they will feel blamed for their relative's disorder by the professional leading the training (Spaniol et al., 1984). In view of how sensitive families are to implications of blame (Hatfield, 1979; Wasow, 1980), pure skill-training approaches will be limited if some families refuse to participate because they will feel blamed and stigmatized by the approach. Finally, these approaches provide almost no training for the advocacy needs of families.

Supportive Approaches

Supportive approaches are interventions primarily designed to enhance the emotional capacity of the family to cope with the stresses of caring for a psychiatrically disabled relative. Typically, family members share their feelings and experiences about caring for their disabled relative. In return, the family is reassured that such care giving is difficult, that they are doing the best they can, and that they do not need to feel guilty. While provision of information and skill training may occur at times, the central goal of support approaches is to alter the emotional state of the participants.

The National Alliance for the Mentally Ill (NAMI) has developed the most widely used support model (Hatfield, 1981; Straw & Young, 1982; Wasow, 1982). NAMI was not developed by professionals in response to the needs of families. Instead, it was developed as a self-help and advocacy group by individuals with psychiatrically disabled relatives (Hatfield, 1981). Since its official founding in 1979, NAMI has grown dramatically and currently is composed of hundreds of local chapters representing more than forty thousand members.

NAMI seems to be able to meet some family needs more successfully than many professionals. It provides families with a powerful vehicle for advocating for changes in the mental health system. Family members also discovered that there is a great deal of comfort to be found in mutual support (Hatfield, 1981). Joining together to share experiences with a common problem seems to be a useful experience for many individuals, and is the basis for many self-help groups (Killilea, 1976; 1982).

NAMI appears to be a successful group, as indicated by its large and growing size. Hatfield (1979) surveyed 79 NAMI and NAMI-like support groups and found that a large majority of the members were satisfied with their groups. Many chapters have become actively involved in political advocacy (Straw & Young, 1982) and some chapters are beginning to provide direct services to psychiatrically disabled individuals (Shifren-Levine & Spaniol, 1985). The core of most groups, however, remains the support/advocacy function.

Some mental health professionals also attempt to provide support to families. One supportive model is reported by Byalin, Jed, and Lehman (1982). The goal is to "enhance the capacity of families of these patients to cope with the stresses of caring for a severely and chronically ill member without overtly attempting to change behavior" (p. 2). The professional visits the family home as a guest and makes no attempt to provide therapy. Instead, two themes are emphasized: first, the family is told that they are cosufferers in a family tragedy rather than the people who caused the tragedy; second, the family is told that mental health professionals have failed to provide significant aid. The family maintains control over the interaction and sets the scheduling and duration of the visit. The results of this approach are encouraging. Not only do families feel comfortable with the model but a small pilot study using the model found that it significantly reduced the hospitalization time of the disabled family member.

Supportive approaches share strengths. First, they meet a need expressed by families. Wasow (1980) found that the most frequently voiced need of families was the need not to be blamed for their relative's disorder. Supportive approaches, whether provided by professionals or by family members themselves, share the ability to relieve some of the guilt, anger, and frustration experienced by families. Second, supportive approaches are nonstigmatizing and relatively unintrusive. For family members who want and need an opportunity to share their experiences with other individuals in similar situations but who do not want skill training or structured educational sessions, a supportive approach provides a nonthreatening alternative.

Supportive approaches also have a serious limitation. If a family wants or needs skills or information that will help them to be more effective care givers or advocates, supportive approaches will probably not be powerful enough to meet their needs. And most family members do need specific skills and information at some time during the course of their care-giving efforts.

Comprehensive Approaches

At least one model has been developed by professionals that is intended to provide information skills and support as parts of a structured and comprehensive intervention (Leff, Berkowitz, Eberbein-Vries, & Sturgeon, 1982). This approach, which is termed "social intervention," is a three-part model. First, families receive four lectures on etiology, symptoms, and prognosis of schizophrenia in an attempt to provide them with basic information. Second, families participate in a multi-family support group that is designed to provide an opportunity to share experiences, problems, and solutions. Finally, families receive up to 25 sessions with a mental health professional. These sessions provide a combination of dynamic insights and teaching of behavioral interventions to families. The results of this approach are encouraging. The relapse rate of disabled individuals whose families participated in this group was only 9 percent over a nine-month period, compared to 50 percent for a control group receiving traditional outpatient treatment.

This approach has the combined strengths (and limitations) of the skills-training and supportive approaches. Despite the comprehensiveness of the approach, client outcome data is not significantly better than less comprehensive approaches. The relapse rate of patients whose families participated in

Anderson's (1983) educational model was also less than 10 percent. Goldstein and Kopeikin's (1981) skill-training approach resulted in an even lower rate of relapse. Although the relapse rates are not provided for their support-only approach, Byalin et al. (1982) show a mean rate of hospitalization for their group over a 12-month period of only 10.3 days, compared to a mean rate of 56.3 days per year for these same individuals during the preceding four years. Thus there is some question as to whether the intense and comprehensive model described by Leff et al. is worth the additional effort.

Summary of Innovative Approaches

When a family with a mentally ill relative comes to a mental health practitioner for services, the practitioner has a wide range of informative skill-building, supportive, or comprehensive interventions from which to choose. However, it is not clear that any of these approaches offers a distinct advantage over the others in client outcome. Each of the models seems to be equally effective in reducing the relapse rate of the mentally ill family member.

There are two possible explanations for the similarity in the effectiveness of the models. First, global outcome indicators such as relapse or recidivism rates may be too broad to capture significant differences between the approaches. Utilization of outcome measures of family dissatisfaction, client satisfaction, client level of functioning, family level of functioning, and stress level may demonstrate some differences between the models in terms of outcome. Second, it may be that each of the models shares a core group of common features, resulting in similar outcomes. Each of the approaches attempts to engage the family in a partnership and gives the family some control over the intervention. Each attempts not to blame the family for the disability of the mentally ill member. Each of the approaches provides either skills, information, or support, or some combination of these services, to help families cope more effectively with their mentally ill relative. The comparable outcomes of all of these models may be explained by arguing that each of them employs a range of strategies that may be independent of a specific causal model of family distress or patient relapse but which somehow relates directly to what families have been saying they want or need from professionals. Professionals should learn and use these approaches in addition to or in place of more traditional therapeutic interventions.

FAMILY COPING

There has been little systematic assessment of the coping strategies employed by families with mentally ill members. The most recent survey is a national survey by Spaniol et al. (1984) of 141 family members who belonged to the National Alliance for the Mentally Ill.

For purposes of data presentation, the responses were collapsed into two groups: families stating that they were coping very inadequately, inadequately, or minimally adequately were designated as "non-copers"; families stating that they were coping adequately or very adequately were designated as "copers." Thirty-five percent of the respondents were categorized as noncopers, while 65 percent were categorized as copers.

Families were asked to state why they might be coping adequately or inadequately with their ill family member. Utilizing a t-test, significant differences were found between coping and noncoping families on each of the reasons surveyed. Copers tended to agree more frequently and noncopers tended to disagree more frequently with the statement that symptoms can be handled at homne ($t = 4.14$, $p < .001$), that medication is working effectively ($t = 4.87$, $p < .001$), that physical aggression is minimal ($t = 255$, $p < .05$), that the costs of care are manageable ($t = 3.29$, $p < .01$), that their emotional support is adequate ($t = 5.09$, $p < .001$), that the information they have is useful for guidance ($t = 2.60$, $p < .05$), and that mental health services are available to them ($t = 2.91$, $p < .01$).

Using the groups designated as copers and noncopers, t-tests were calculated on items asking about the adequacy of information that families receive on mental health services and treatment. Results indicated that there were significant differences for the copers and noncopers on several items. Copers tended to perceive themselves as having enough information, and noncopers tended to perceive themselves as having not enough information for coping regarding the causes of schizophrenia ($t = 2.19$, $p < .05$), the diagnosis of schizophrenia ($t = 1.99$, $p < .05$), the effects of treatment services ($t = 2.61$, $p < .05$), coping skills for themselves ($t = 3.51$, $p < .001$), stress management for themselves ($t = 3.26$, $p < .01$) and community resources ($t = 2.55$, $p < .05$). In contrast, there was no significant difference between the copers and the noncopers on whether they had enough information on medication management and genetic counseling. Both copers and noncopers tended to agree that they lacked adequate information on these last two items.

An analysis was made of the relationship between coping ability and a family's ability to manage their disabled family member's behavior. Utilizing a t-test, a significant difference was found between the copers and noncopers ($t = 3.37$, $df = 135$, $p < .001$). The copers reported feeling more capable of managing their disabled family member's behavior. It is important to note, however, that even the copers did not feel completely capable of managing their disabled family member's behavior.

It was hypothesized that involvement of the family respondent in face-to-face counseling might be related to a family's ability to cope. There was no significant difference between the copers and the noncopers with respect to the frequency of face-to-face counseling during the twelve months preceding the survey ($\times 2 = 2.08$, $p < .359$). However, since the frequency of counseling was quite limited for both groups, this may not be an adequate test of the efficacy of counseling.

Respondents were also asked about their level of satisfaction with the present living arrangements of their disabled family member. Forty-eight percent indicated that they were pleased or extremely pleased with these arrangements, while 31 percent reported they were displeased or extremely displeased. In the coping survey sample, 27 percent of the disabled family members lived at home.

Hatfield (1981) has also studied the coping responses of 30 parents, all members of a self-help group for parents of the mentally ill. This study is limited primarily by the select nature of respondents, who were characterized by high educational attainment, family income over $20,000, stable marriage, and suburban living. The study was carried out over a 30-month period, and Hatfield used a focused interview schedule and quarterly reports to record the data.

Hatfield found that coping styles could be distinguished between the effective and ineffective coping parents. The effectively coping parents were able to gain a sense of emotional mastery, develop cognitive skills, and attain a sense of self-fulfillment. These parents, while initially shocked and upset, were able to accept their situation and face it realistically. They also engaged in an avid search for information that would help their cause. These parents felt able to manage their offsprings' behavior. In terms of their personal needs, they were able to find time to attend to themselves.

The ineffectively coping group was characterized by a crisis-oriented, reactive approach to their situation. They eventually became emotionally burdened and exhausted. They also engaged in an avid search for information, but they were unable to use the information to develop effective coping strategies. These parents also had fewer outside interests than the effectively coping groups. The most effectively coping families had older offspring who had been ill longer, exhibited lower psychosocial functioning, and were frequently institutionalized. The least effectively coping families had younger offspring with a shorter duration of illness and higher functioning level, and the offspring usually lived in the community.

Thompson and Doll (1982) interviewed 125 family caregivers six months after patients returned home to determine "how families handle the burdens of coping in their care-giving role." Findings revealed that half of the relatives provided extra supervision, approximately one-third acknowledged that they neglected responsibilities to other family members, and more than one-third experienced added financial burden. A majority of relatives expressed a feeling of being overloaded, 46 percent expressed a feeling of being trapped and 13 percent expressed intense resentment. Despite these perceived burdens, few relatives (7%) wished for greater emotional distance or the total exclusion of the patient from their lives.

Summary of Family Coping

In summary, three points are clear. First, families with mentally ill members are often stressed, burdened, and overwhelmed by their caretaking role. However, in spite of the pressures, most families cope reasonably well. They are needy but not helpless. Second, families cope well if they have better information about mental illness, better emotional support, better success with psychiatric medication, less financial burden, more available mental health services, and less trouble with physical aggression. Professionals would be well advised to help families with these factors. Third, families already have a broad range of coping strategies that they report to be effective. Professionals should listen to and learn from these families and their wealth of experience and practical expertise.

RESEARCH DIRECTIONS

The research findings discussed in this paper have been based primarily on survey research strategies. Clearly, there is a need to increase the use of other types of research methodologies with families. In addition to use of more experimental or controlled approaches, we need more intensive approaches, such as participant-observation or extensive interviews. While the question of methodology is important, it is not quite as critical as the need to ask additional key questions with respect to families. The questions are especially critical now, because the models we have for understanding families of the mentally ill are being challenged by families and by much of the research discussed in this paper. There is a need for new understandings and new models to meet the challenge and to fill the void left by inadequate understandings and inappropriate models. Areas of needed research include:

- Family stress and family burden

- Stages of adjustment of the family to the crises of mental illness in a family member
- Siblings of the mentally ill
- Practitioner attitudes and expectations
- The role of the family in the rehabilitation of their disabled family member
- Cross-cultural issues and comparisons
- Coping strengths of families
- Families and the advocacy process
- Professional/family relationships
- The impact of training professionals to work with families

There is extensive literature on families with a physically disabled person. Professional attitudes toward and support for those families is quite different than professional attitudes toward and support for families with a mentally ill member. The strong advocacy of families of the physically disabled and extensive research on their experience has provided the needed information and professional support that families of the mentally ill lack. Advocacy has become a reality for families of the mentally ill. Our research effort has only begun.

CONCLUDING COMMENTS

The research findings summarized in this paper represent a significant shift in professional thinking about families with mentally ill members. This shift has six main points.

1. In many cases, families have become the primary care givers for their mentally ill family member. Families are not satisfied with this situation, and they feel abandoned by the mental health system.
2. Families should be seen as reactors to the mental illness of one of their members rather than the cause of the disorder.
3. Families with mentally ill members need special skills, information, and support in their care-giving efforts. Meeting these needs benefits the entire family, including the ill family member.

4. Traditional family therapy is not a service that is desired by most families with mentally ill members.
5. Families with mentally ill members have many strengths, and many report that they are coping adequately with their ill member.
6. Mental health professionals should be educators and consultants to families with mentally ill members. Professionals should provide the skills, information, and support that families need to cope with and care for their ill family members.

Although a growing body of research supports these conclusions, training programs for mental health professionals have been slow to integrate this knowledge into the academic curriculum. Our schools must incorporate the findings of this research into introductory courses in mental health, social work, community mental health, psychology, counseling, and family therapy. Such an education will prepare professionals to give families with mentally ill members the assistance they need.

This paper was written with the support of NIHR Grant No. G008005486.

REFERENCES

Anderson, C. (1983). A Psychoeducational program for families of patients with schizophrenia. In W. McFarlane (Ed.), *Family therapy in schizophrenia.* New York: Guildford Press.

Anderson, C., Hogarty, G., & Reiss, D. (1980). Family treatment of adult schizophrenia patients: A Psychoeducational approach. *Schizophrenia Bulletin, 6*(3), 490-505.

Anderson, C., Hogarty, G., & Reiss, D. (1981). The psychoeducational family treatment of schizophrenia. In M. Goldstein (Ed.), *New directions for mental health services: New developments in interventions with families of schizophrenics,* No. 12. San Francisco: Jossey-Bass.

Arieti, S. (1974) *Interpretation of schizophrenia* (2nd Edition). New York: Basic Books.

Bateson, G., Jackson, D., Haley, J., & Weakland, J. (1956). Toward a theory of schizophrenia. *Behavioral Science, 1*(4), 251-264.

Beels, C. & McFarlane, W. (1982). Family treatment of schizophrenia: Background and state of the art. *Hospital and Community Psychiatry, 1,* 541-550.

Bernheim, K., Lewine, R., & Beale, C. (1982). *The caring family: Living with chronic mental illness.* New York: Random House.

Bowen, M. (1960). A family concept of schizophrenia. In D.D. Jackson (Ed.), *The etiology of schizophrenia.* New York: Basic Books.

Brown, G., Birley, J., & Wing, J. (1987). Influence of family life on the course of schizophrenic disorders: A replication. *British Journal of Psychiatry, 121,* 241-258.

Byalin, K., Jed, J. & Lehamn, S. (1982). Family intervention with treatment-refractory chronic schizophrenics. Paper presented at 20th International Congress of Applied Psychology, Edinburgh, Scotland.

Creer, C. & Wing, J. (1974). *Schizophrenia at home.* London: Institute of Psychiatry.

Dincin, J., Selleck, W., & Steicker, S. (1978). Restructuring parental attitudes: Working with parents of the adult mentally ill. *Schizophrenia Bulletin, 4,* 597-608.

Doll, W. (1976). Family coping with the mentally ill: An unanticipated problem of deinstitutionalization. *Hospital and Community Psychiatry, 27*(3), 183-185.

Falloon, I., Boyde, J., McGill, C., Razani, J., Moss, H., & Gilderman, A. (1982). Family management in the prevention of exacerbations of schizophrenia: A controlled study. *New England Journal of Medicine, 306,*1437-1440.

Falloon, I. (1981). Liberman, R., Lillie, F., & Vaughn, C. (1981). Family therapy of schizophrenics with high risk of relapse. *Family Process, 20,* 211-221.

Fromm-Reichman, F. (1948). Notes on the development of treatment of schizophrenics by psychoanalytic psychotherapy. *Psychiatry, 11,* 263-273.

Goldman, H. (1982). Mental Illness and family burden: A public health perspective. *Hospital and Community Psychiatry, 33*(7), 557-559.

Goldman, H. & Gatozzi, A. (1981). Defining and counting the chronically mentally ill. *Hospital and Community Psychiatry, 32*(1) 21-27.

Goldstein, M. & Kopeikin, H. (1981). Short- and long-term effects of combining drug and family therapy. In M.J. Goldstein (Ed.), *New directions for mental health services: New developments in interventions with families of schizophrenics,* No. 12. San Francisco: Jossey-Bass.

Hatfield, A. (1978). Psychological costs of schizophrenia to the family. *Social Casework, 23,* 355-359.

Hatfield, A. (1979). The family as a partner in the treatment of mental illness. *Hospital and Community Psychiatry, 30,* 338-340.

Hatfield, A. (1981). Self-help groups for families of the mentally ill. *Social Casework, 26,* 408-413.

Hatfield, A., Fierstein, R., & Johnson, D. (1983). Meeting the needs of families of the psychiatrically disabled. *Psychosocial Rehabilitation Journal, 6*(1), 27-40.

Hatfield, A. (1983). What families want from family therapists. In W. McFarlane (Ed.), *Family Therapy in Schizophrenia.* New York: Guildford Press.

Hatfield, A. (1984). Coping with mental illness in the family: The family guide. Available from the National Alliance for the Mentally Ill.

Hirsch, S. & Leff, J. (1985). *Abnormalities in the parents of schizophrenics.* London: Oxford University Press.

Holden, D. & Lewine, R. (1982). How families evaluate mental health professionals, resources and effects of illness.*Schizophrenia Bulletin, 8*(4), 626-633.

Hyde, A. (1980). Living with schizophrenia. Chicago: Contemporary Books, Inc.

Jung, H., Spaniol, L., & Anthony, W. (1983). Family coping and schizophrenia. Available from the Boston University Center for Rehabilitation Research and Training in Mental Health.

Hogarty, G., Goldberg, S., & Schooler, N. (1975). Drug and sociotherapy in the aftercare of schizophrenia: A review. In M. Greenblatt (Ed.), *Drugs in combination with other therapy*. New York: Grune and Stratton, Inc.

Killilea, M. (1976). Mutual help organizations: Interpretations in the literature. In G. Kaplan & M. Killilea (Eds.), *Support systems and mutual help*. New York: Grune & Stratton.

Killilea, M. (1982). Interaction of crisis theory, coping strategies and social support systems. In H.C. Schulberg and M. Killilea (Eds.), *The modern practice of community mental health*. San Francisco: Jossey-Bass.

Kint, M. (1978). Schizophrenia is a family affair: Problems of families in coping with schizophrenia. *Journal of Orthomolecular Psychiatry, 4,* 236-246.

Kopeikin, H., Marshall, V., & Goldstein, M. (1983). Stages and impact of crisis-oriented family therapy in the aftercare of acute schizophrenia. In W. McFarlane (Ed.), *Family therapy in schizophrenia*. New York: Guilford Press.

Kreisman, D. & Joy, V. (1974). Family response to the mental illness of relatives: A review of the literature. *Schizophrenia Bulletin, 10,* 34-57.

Lamb, R. & Oilphant, E. (1978). Schizophrenia through the eyes of families. *Hospital and Community Psychiatry, 9*(12), 803-806.

Leff, J., Kuipers, L., Berkowitz, R., Eberbein-Vries, R., & Sturgeon, D. (1982). Controlled trial of social intervention in the families of schizophrenic patients. *British Journal of Psychiatry, 141,* 121-134.

Leff, J. & Vaughn, C. (1980). The interaction of life events and relatives' expressed emotion in schizophrenia and depressive neurosis. *British Journal of Psychiatry, 136,* 146-153.

Liberman, R., Wallace, C., Vaughn, C., & Snyder, K. (1979). Social and family factors in the course of schizophrenia. Paper presented at the Conference on Psychotherapy of Schizophrenia: Current Status and New Directions. New Haven, Conn.: Yale University School of Medicine.

Liberman, R., Aitchison, R., & Falloon, J. (1979). Family therapy in schizophrenia: Syllabus for therapists. Unpublished manuscript. Available from Mental Health Clinical Research Center for the Study of Schizophrenia, Camarillo/UCLA Research Program, Box A, Camarillo, 93010.

Lidz, T. (1970). Schizophrenia and the family. *Psychiatry, 21,* 21-27.

Messer, A. (1970). *The individual in his family: An adaptive study*. Springfield, Ill.: Charles Thomas.

Minkoff, K. (1979). A map of chronic mental patients. In J. Talbott (Ed.), *The chronic mental patient*. Washington, D.C.: American Psychiatric Association, 11-37.

Messer, A. (1970). *The individual in his family: An adaptation study*. Springfield, Ill.: Thomas.

May, P., Tuma, H., & Dixon, W. (1976). Schizophrenia: A follow-up study of the results of five forms of treatment. *Archives of General Psychiatry, 33,* 474-478.

O'Connor, M. (1983). An investigation of family burden in the parents of schizophrenic patients. Unpublished master's thesis, Boston University, School of Nursing.

Park, C. & Shapiro, L. (1976). *You are not alone: Understanding and dealing with mental illness.* Boston: Little, Brown & Co.

Plummer, E., Thornton, J., Seeman, M., & Littman, S. (1981). Coping with schizophrenia: A group approach with relatives. *Journal of Psychiatric Treatment and Evaluation, 3,* 257-262.

Shifren-Levine, I. & Spaniol, L. (1985). The role of families of the severely mentally ill in the development of community support services. *Psychosocial Rehabilitation Journal, 8*(4), 83-94.

Spaniol, L., Zipple, A., & FitzGerald, S. (1984a). How professionals can share power with families: A practical approach to working with families of the mentally ill. *Psychosocial Rehabilitation Journal, 8*(2), 77-84.

Spaniol, L., Jung, H., Zipple, A., & FitzGerald, S. (1984b). Families as a central resource in the rehabilitation of the severely psychiatrically disabled: Report of a national survey. Submitted for publication.

Straw, P. & Young, B. Awakenings: A self-help group organization kit. Available from National Alliance for the Mentally Ill, 1901 N. Ft. Myer Drive, #500, Arlington, VA 22209.

Terkelsen, K. (1983). Schizophrenia and the family, II. Adverse effects of family therapy. *Family Process, 22,* 191-200.

Thompson, E. & Doll, W. (1982). The burden of families coping with mental illness: An invisible crisis. *Family Relations, 31,*379-388.

Torrey, E. (1983). *Surviving schizophrenia: A family manual.* Cambridge, MA: Harper and Row.

Walsh, M. (1985). *Schizophrenia: Straight talk for family and friends.* New York: William Morrow and Company.

Wasow, M. (1980). Professionals have hurt us. Parents of schizophrenics speak out. Unpublished manuscript. Available from M. Wasow, Mt. Sinai Medical Center, 950 N. 12th St., P.O. Box 342, Milwaukee, WI 53201.

Wasow, M. (1982). *Coping with schizophrenia: A survival manual for parents, relatives, and friends.* Palo Alto: Science and Behavior Books, Inc.

Willis, M. (1982). The impact of schizophrenia on families: One mother's point of view. *Schizophrenia Bulletin, 8*(4), 617-619.

Wynne, L., Ryckoff, I., Day, J., & Hirsch, S. (1958). Pseudomutuality in the family relations of schizophrenics. *Psychiatry, 21,* 205-220.

Chapter 4

Information Needs of Social Work Practitioners Working With Psychiatrically Disabled Persons

David P. Moxley

The practice terrain of social workers working with people who have psychiatric disabilities is rapidly changing. This is especially true in relation to emerging treatment and rehabilitation technologies and methods of organizing and delivering care (Gordon & Gordon, 1981). Rapid stabilization, case management approaches, continua of residential alternatives, vocational development services, and structured skill-building strategies are just some of the practice technologies which are being introduced into community-based care (Barofsky & Budson, 1983; Kanter, 1985).

The psychiatric institution is on the wane as the primary site of care, while new settings, such as decentralized community support services and specialized psychosocial rehabilitation centers, are being created to respond to the community living needs of people with psychiatric disabilities. As systems of community-based care are more able to respond comprehensively to the needs of people with psychiatric disabilities, these systems are able to assume many of the institutions' functions.

Epidemiological estimates indicate the increasing significance of community-service systems in the provision of care. The number of people with severe psychiatric disability living in the community is now close to the number that is institutionalized. Goldman (1984) estimates that 900,000 people live within the confines of institutions, while 800,000 people with severe disabilities live within community settings. Adding those with

83

moderate disability, the size of the community population expands to approximately 1,500,000.

Of the many functions served by mental hospitals that Bachrach (1976) has identified, several are now key aspects of community-based systems: long-term care to people with severe disabilities, emergency psychiatric care for people experiencing acute episodes, protection of the person from victimization, a supervised residential setting, and ongoing monitoring of the course of the person's illness.

This paper will outline some of the significant information needs of social workers practicing within the field of psychiatric rehabilitation. In particular, it will emphasize information that will improve the delivery of social work services within community-based systems of care. By providing such information, researchers can make major contributions to social work within this field of practice.

RELEVANT AREAS OF PRACTICE INFORMATION

To address the information needs of social workers practicing in the field of psychiatric rehabilitation, researchers should focus on three substantive areas. The first area is the effectiveness of various approaches to organizing the care of people who have psychiatric disability. It involves examining alternative organizational auspices for the delivery of care.

The second area should focus on approaches to service delivery and the effectiveness of these approaches in improving the social functioning of people with psychiatric disabilities. In this area it is important to evaluate the impact of consumer and family involvement on the social functioning of the client, analyzing approaches to case management, evaluating the impact of long-term case management on the social functioning of the client, and evaluating the impact of social support strategies on successful community living. Information on effective methods of outreach and retention is also critically needed within this area.

A third area is the clinical nature of psychiatric disability. Important issues here are the usefulness of the concept of chronicity and a better differentiation of the subpopulations of those with psychiatric disability. These issues are discussed below.

INFORMATION PERTAINING TO THE ORGANIZATIONAL AUSPICES OF CARE

Researchers can make a significant contribution to our understanding of how different organizational auspices of care for people with psychiatric disabilities influence treatment outcomes. A major issue is whether organizations that specialize in responding to the needs of the psychiatrically disabled are more effective than those providing general mental health services.

Given a major commitment to the delivery of psychotherapeutic services, community mental health centers may not be the best organizational base for the delivery of care to people who can have significant functional problems in community living. I have emphasized elsewhere that programs seeking to serve this population should do so in a specialized way so as to reduce competing demands on the allocation of agency resources.

> Historically, mentally disabled persons have had to compete with other groups in accessing human services. Providers have also had to make programmatic choices about whether to serve the severely mentally disabled or to serve less severely disabled groups. Since the mentally ill tend not to make attractive clients, tend to make slow progress, and tend to be difficult to motivate, many professionals gravitate toward serving less impaired people. By moving towards specialization, programs prioritize, the importance of caring for this group and introduce more equity in the sense that more resources are invested in those with severe disabilities as compared to persons with less severe problems (Moxley, 1984, p. 5).

These observations are based on my own practice experience and have not been validated by empirical research. Through service-system research, social work investigators can begin to examine outcomes that are related to different approaches to the organization of care. Such alternatives can include:

1. *Psychosocial rehabilitation centers* that place a primary focus on serving the chronically mentally ill through the provision of work, educational, residential, and socialization opportunities.

2. *Comprehensive rehabilitation centers* that assist clients to reduce the significance of their disabilities through goal-directed learning of skills relevant to community living. In addition, such centers seek to integrate vocational evaluation, work activities, and employment services with other critical spheres of living such as housing, socialization, and the development of leisure interests.

3. *Independent living centers* that provide an array of concrete services as well as referral, service coordination, and case management activities all designed to foster community living of persons with severe disabilities. The model is grounded in substantial consumer involvement, governance and administration (DeLoach, Wilkins & Walker, 1983; Frieden, Richards, Cole & Bailey, 1979).

4. *Social health maintenance organizations* that integrate social, health, medical, and psychological services within one provider system. This provider assumes comprehensive responsibility for a full range of service delivery, which is financed through a capitation rate. Elderplan, a social health maintenance organization for the elderly, focuses on identifying frail elderly people who are at risk of institutionalization. Through a case management system, a long-term care plan is formulated that combines in-home and community services as alternatives to nursing homes (Alternative Design Newsletter, 1984).

Such a model can be applied to those who have disabilities as a result of mental illness. They are often faced with lack of service integration and lack of access, and are often in jeopardy of placement in restrictive settings. The positive aspect of the social health maintenance organization is that it provides an incentive to serve a so-called difficult and "unattractive" population. The social health maintenance approach is consistent with Mechanic's (1979) recommendation that a large agency or consortium of agencies accept full responsibility for providing the full spectrum of hospital, community services, and support structures required by people with major psychiatric disabilities.

This type of research can take different forms. Researchers may pursue this line of investigation through explanatory surveys that explore treatment outcomes across many types of organizational auspices. An exemplar of this research is Tessler and Goldman's work (1982) on evaluating NIMH-sponsored community support programs. Alternatively, demonstration research would be very valuable in this area. Through the design and implementation of pilot demonstrations, investigators can examine the impact of such alternative models on the social functioning and psychiatric status of participants.

INFORMATION PERTAINING TO SERVICE DELIVERY AND PROFESSIONAL PRACTICE

Practice-relevant research must provide information on optimal approaches to the delivery of services. A number of issues have not received systematic attention by researchers: consumer and family involvement, social support in community living, case management, and outreach and retention. Each issue is discussed below.

Evaluating the Impact of Consumer and Family Involvement

A major issue in the field of psychiatric disability is the involvement of consumers and family members in the provision of services. Such involvement now includes consumer and family participation in the planning of services, the involvement of consumers in the governance of programs, and the involvement of consumers as service providers (Smith et al., 1984).

Consumer and family involvement has been encouraged through the dissemination of psychosocial rehabilitation principles that incorporate a strong consumer involvement ideology

(Hatfield, 1981). In Ohio a statewide consumer network is in its early stages of development, while special block grants, made available by the Ohio Department of Mental Health, have been provided to develop consumer-operated drop-in centers and social clubs in key areas of the state. Families are also organizing self-help groups. Local family groups in Ohio have formed the statewide Ohio Family Coalition, which is dedicated to legislative, educational, vocational, and rehabilitation goals. The message being sent to professionals by consumers and families is that they want to have input into many aspects of care, including the formulation of treatment plans, the provision of treatment, and the development of service systems.

Some professionals are not comfortable with such involvement and do not welcome it. A pressing research issue is whether the involvement of family members and consumers enhances the positive effects of treatment or whether it has negative effects. Does consumer involvement make a difference in treatment outcomes? What are the long-range effects of consumer involvement? Do different forms of consumer involvement lead to different outcomes? These questions must be creatively approached by researchers, and they may require the evaluation of demonstration projects, random assignment to different conditions or levels of involvement, or the systematic evaluation of self-help efforts.

Rappaport and his colleagues (1985) are demonstrating that researchers can conduct longitudinal research of self-help efforts in collaboration with consumers. The evaluation of GROW, which consists of locally organized support groups of people who are experiencing mental illness, makes use of a "resource collaborator" model. The overall research approach has been defined and developed through the joint collaboration of researchers and GROW members.

The Impact of Social Support on Community Living

It is important to provide enriched social support to people with mental disability. Outcome research can provide information on (1) whether enriched social support leads to more successful community living and even movement towards independent living, and (2) whether programming delivered through community-based systems leads to the development of nonprofessional support systems for people with psychiatric disabilities.

What is the role of social support in the lives of people with psychiatric disabilities? From my practice experience, I have found that it is easy for clients to become entrenched in professional support systems. My practice experience also tells me that nonprofessional sources of support can assist clients in negotiating crises, staying out of the hospital, and avoiding isolation.

Research on social support that is mediated through the social networks of clients is critical, especially on the effects of social network resources in preventing decompensation, how to retain people in care, and avoiding crises and hospitalizations. Another issue for research is the extent to which community programming for people with psychiatric disabilities leads to the development of nonprofessional support systems. Do skill building programs lead to clients' enhanced ability to develop supportive social networks? Does case management lead to increased social integration? Does family education lead to more effective support systems for clients? These questions deal with an ongoing dilemma of service delivery. While professionals are providing care within community settings, we must be certain that clients are indeed developing alternative support systems. If we are not achieving such outcomes, we may be only developing decentralized institutions within our communities.

Research on Case Management

Case management is certainly a concept which is in "good currency." Many agencies are establishing case management services, but theory, conceptualization, and effectiveness data are far behind practice.

A case management system is vital for integrating services at the level of the client. In a decentralized community system of care, achieving continuity, follow-through, and comprehensiveness is too complex for the individual consumer. Some entity—be it an individual professional or a multidisciplinary team—must assume responsibility for the overall assessment of need, planning of care, and monitoring and evaluating service provision.

There is a critical need for basic information on case management. Practitioners need information at the operational level. What are different models of case management? What are the best job designs for case managers? What skills are necessary for effective case management? And how can an administrator measure the productivity of a case manager?

A large-scale survey of case management practices similar to Steinberg and Carter's survey (1983) of case management in the field of aging is needed. Data collection on case management models, implementation issues, administrative practices, and human resource practices would define the state of the art. The identification of exemplars through selected in-depth case studies can provide models for replication.

Effectiveness studies evaluating the impact of case management on the social functioning and social integration of clients are also critically needed. It is important to implement "model" approaches, but it is also critical to evaluate the impact of these models. These studies should focus on both intended and unintended effects. Investigation of the latter is important to a practitioner's understanding of whether case management programs can inadvertently increase client dependency or create utilization barriers by adding another layer of administrative authority to community programs.

Effectiveness studies can compare case management to other forms of social treatment such as psychotherapy or office-based casework. A comparison of different models or intensities of case management can also be the focus of such studies.

Studies that examine the effectiveness of case management must consider the population served by community systems. People with psychiatric disabilities have long-term needs which cut across multiple delivery systems. A fruitful investigation of the impact of case management should be undertaken on a longitudinal basis. In addition, outcome studies focusing on the impact of case management on clients, their support systems, and the delivery of human services are vital to a thorough understanding of the contribution that case management can make to the psychiatric rehabilitation of clients.

Methods of Outreach and Retention

Another important issue of psychiatric rehabilitation is the emphasis placed on outreach as a means of retaining people within community-based systems of care or of bringing new clients into these systems. Outreach is the screening and assessing of clients in natural settings and delivering care in these settings. Innovation is possible in how social workers deliver outreach services, and information on the effectiveness of different outreach strategies and their impact on different client populations is needed.

These investigations can take the form of quasi-experiments involving simple interventions, such as mailing greeting cards to clients reminding them of scheduled appointments. More complex studies can provide information on ways to increase the retention of clients with histories of high recidivism. Investigators can gauge the impact of service provision within home settings, the use of mobile treatment teams that follow clients into community settings, or behavioral programs which are designed to increase the self-administration of medication (Bond et al., 1984).

The development of effective outreach programs must be based on an understanding of how clients utilize health care. Identifying the conditions under which some clients make use of services while others do not can provide information for planning outreach efforts. Given the financial and personal costs of recidivism, a program of research in this area may result in substantial benefits to both clients and professionals.

INFORMATION PERTAINING TO THE CLINICAL NATURE OF PSYCHIATRIC DISABILITY

Practitioners and researchers alike are recognizing that the target population of the chronically mentally ill is not homogeneous but diverse. The chronic schizophrenic population that accounted for the early waves of deinstitutionalization, and which presented significant motivational and skill deficits, is now aging. Practitioners are experiencing an influx of a different population that has been diverted from long-term hospitalization: younger people who present severe conduct and behavioral problems (Pepper & Rygliewicz, 1984). This new population may not fit easily into the old community support components designed for people who are more passive. The emerging population, which presents problems of behavioral control and behavioral management, is a significant contrast to the older population, which primarily needed supportive service components. Many programs are serving people who present behavioral problems and who consume a significant portion of staff time and energy (Pepper et al., 1984).

We cannot continue to treat the chronically mentally ill as an undifferentiated target population, but must recognize the heterogeneity of this group. Implications for differential service design and delivery are significant. Level of structure, amount of stimulation, focus of the programming, and the degree of assertiveness in outreach and follow-along may all need to be considered when differentiating programs for those with motivational and skill deficits from those serving persons who present behavioral, conduct, and law-enforcement problems.

In addition to research that helps differentiate clinical characteristics of people with major psychiatric disabilities, investigation into the concept of chronicity may contribute to the development of relevant community programs. Longitudinal analyses of the community status of people with severe disabilities are rare. Data on whether a person remains "chronically" disabled and on long-range developmental outcomes related to treatment or no treatment needs to be generated within the field.

It is not clear whether some of the chronic conditions practitioners observe are related to illness or to iatrogenic effects of program participation. What is needed is sensitive longitudinal research focusing on the intended and unintended effects of our community-support and treatment programs.

CONCLUSION

Social work has much to contribute to the field of psychiatric rehabilitation. Its historical emphasis on self-determination and empowerment are compatible with the emerging emphasis on consumer involvement in the field. Working with lay and informal helpers has been a key aspect of social work practice and certainly intersects with the interest in developing the social support and social networks of people with psychiatric disabilities. We do not have to search far to identify commonalities between social work practice and psychiatric rehabilitation. Strengthening our own research efforts can strengthen the partnership bettween social work and the field of psychiatric rehabilitation.

A strategic plan for social work research in this field must be broad. On one level, research should challenge philosophical assumptions by providing empirical evaluations of the effects of programs. On another level, social work research can assist practitioners in validating state-of-the-art practices and in identifying exemplars of social work practice that can be adapted or replicated in the field of psychiatric rehabilitation. Research and development efforts can also provide critical input into the formulation of practice technologies that are effective in serving people with major psychiatric disabilities.

Research can serve the pivotal function of mediating between theory and practice. Through the implementation of a relevant research agenda, social workers can make significant contributions to more effective service delivery for people who are experiencing psychiatric disabilities and related problems in social functioning.

REFERENCES

Alternative design newsletter, Elderplan issue. (1984). Fairfax, Va.: Pralon.

Bachrach, L. (1976). *Deinstitutionalization: An analytical review and sociological perspective.* Rockville, MD.: National Institute of Mental Health.

Barofsky, I. & Budson, R. (1983). *The chronic psychiatric patient in the community: Principles of treatment.* Jamaica, New York: Spectrum.

Bond, G., Dincin, J. et al. (1984). The effectiveness of psychiatric rehabilitation: A summary of research at Thresholds. *Psychosocial Rehabilitation Journal,* 7(4), 6-23.

DeLoach, C., Wilkins, R., & Walker, G. (1983). *Independent living: Philosophy, process, and services.* Baltimore: University Park Press.

Frieden, L., Richards, L., Cole, J. & Bailey, D. (1979). *ILRU source book: Technical assistance manual on independent living.* Houston: The Institute for Rehabilitation & Research.

Gordon, R. & Gorden, K. (1981). *Systems of treatment for the mentally ill: Filling the gaps.* New York: Grune & Stratton.

Hatfield, A. (1981). Self-help groups for families of the mentally ill. *Social Work, 26,* 408-413.

Kanter, J. (Ed.) (1985). *New directions for mental health services: Clinical issues in treating the chronic mentally ill,* No. 27. San Francisco: Jossey-Bass.

Mechanic, D. (1979). *Future issues in health care: Social policy and the rationing of medical services.* New York: Free Press.

Moxley, D. (1984). Service delivery to the severely mentally disabled: Implications for social work education and practice. Paper presented at the Conference on Educating Social Workers for Work with Chronically Mentally Ill Persons. Washington, D.C. Council on Social Work Education.

Pepper, B. & Ryglewicz, H. (Eds.) (1984). *New directions for mental health services: Advances in treating the young adult chronic patient, No. 21.* San Francisco: Jossey-Bass, 1984.

Rappaport, J., Seidman, E., Toro, P. et al. (1985). Collaborative research with a mutual help organization. *Social Policy, 15*(3), 12-14.

Smith, M., Brown, D., Gibbs, L. et al. (1984). Client involvement in psychosocial rehabilitation. *Psychosocial Rehabilitation Journal, 8*(1), 35-43.

Stein, L. & Test, M.A. (1982). Community treatment of the young adult patient. In B. Pepper & H. Ryglewicz (Eds.), *New directions for mental health services: The young adult chronic patient,* No. 14. San Francisco: Jossey-Bass.

Steinberg, R. & Carter, G. (1983). *Case management and the elderly.* Toronto: Lexington Books.

Tessler, R. & Goldman, H. (1982). *The chronically mentally ill: Assessing community support programs.* Cambridge, MA: Balinger.

Turner, J. & TenHoor, W. (1978). The NIMH community support program: Pilot approach to a needed social reform. *Schizophrenia Bulletin, 4,* 319-349.

Chapter 5

Research in Mental Retardation: Some Relevant Issues for Researchers in Chronic Mental Illness

Lynn McDonald-Wikler and Michael Edwards

People with chronic mental illness and people with mental retardation have been affected by the process of deinstitutionalization over the last decade. Both populations have problems of chronic dependency largely due to disabilities in processing information and to related deficits in social skills. Although the two groups have similar dependencies and service needs, researchers, practitioners, and policy makers historicaly have not crossed over to work with one another. Instead, separate bodies of expertise have coexisted. This paper will summarize several research issues and methodologies used in the field of mental retardation that may have utility for social work researchers in the area of chronic mental illness. The paper will focus particularly on issues relevant to the challenge of self-sufficiency in community living.

There is a long history of research in mental retardation that in some respects is ahead of the work in chronic mental illness. This may reflect in part the fact that in attempting to meet the service needs of people with mental retardation there has been less emphasis on medical diagnostic approaches and more on approaches concerned with the adaptive behavior of the individual in the social environment. Research on mental retardation has increasingly targeted the whole personality and its social circumstances rather than the specific intellectual deficit. The lack of exchange between these two areas of research has perhaps been maintained by the fact that both are fringe areas in the medical and social scientific worlds, thereby encouraging the researchers in each field to emphasize the legitimacy of their own specialties. The two areas also follow separate tracks for funding of research and for the services that apply the results of the research. Finally, a desire to avoid compounding the public's confusion of mental retardation with mental illness has been a further underlying factor in keeping researchers in their own camps. This paper will attempt to bridge these gaps by reviewing some research on people with mental retardation and their social context in an attempt to pinpoint some issues and methodological approaches that may be useful to researchers in the field of the chronically mentally ill.

There are several similarities between people with mental retardation and those with chronic mental illness. First, they share the fact that their problems are attributable to a dysfunction located in the brain, as opposed to other "deviant" groups such as the physically handicapped or delinquents. Second, both populations have experienced a period in which services were dominated by institutional placements, followed by a current public policy that espouses community care. Third, both have been provided services that were based initially on diagnosis and etiology and which have changed their emphasis to one of behavioral social assessment and intervention (although, as noted above, the time frame for the two groups has been different). Fourth, both groups are characterized by chronic dependency.

The shared trait of chronic dependency is significant. It has been the focus of much of the current research in mental retardation, and it is the main characteristic in determining kinds of services that each population needs. Chronic dependency is the issue that most interests social work researchers in the commonalities of these populations. Chronic dependency will therefore be used in this chapter as the organizing concept in reviewing the research literature. As a research subject, the concept can be broken down into three areas:

1. The personal characteristics of the mentally retarded person that promote self-sufficiency.
2. The characteristics of carers and how they promote self-sufficiency.
3. The interaction, or fit, between personal characteristics and carer characteristics as they relate to self-sufficiency.

The paper will consider research and related service developments in mental retardation that may interest researchers of services for the chronically mentally ill population.

THE PERSONAL CHARACTERISTICS OF THE MENTALLY RETARDED PERSON

In identifying the personal characteristics of mentally retarded people that determine their ability to be self-sufficient, researchers have progressively refined their conceptual framework.

Demise of the IQ Measure

In the late 1960s, the validity of IQ measures was brought into question, and it was found that IQ alone was an inadequate predictor of important outcomes such as self-sufficiency in the community, propensity to become institutionalized, development of self-help skills, and employability. However, it was found that if measures of adaptive behavior were included, predictive powers increased. In 1965 the American Association on Mental Deficiency altered the diagnosis of mental retardation to include not only a substandard IQ but also substandard adaptive behavior based on a scale developed by Nihira et al. (1973). In most research studies today, IQ scores alone are not considered acceptable descriptors of a sample of mentally retarded subjects. In addition, federal legislation has defined access to services on the basis of five criteria, none of which includes IQ or even diagnoses of mental retardation, cerebral palsy, or autism (Summer, 1981). Instead, developmental disability is defined by the Federal Developmental Disabilities Act of 1984 as a severe, chronic disability of a person that:

- is attributable to a mental or physical impairment or combination of mental and physical impairments;
- is manifested before the person attains age of 22;
- is likely to continue indefinitely;
- results in substantial functional limitations in three or more of the following areas of major life activity: self care, receptive and expressive language, learning mobility, self-direction, capacity for independent living, and economic self-sufficiency;
- reflects the person's need for a combination and sequence of special, interdisciplinary, or generic care, treatment, or other services that are of lifelong or extended duration and are individually planned and coordinated.

There has been a substantial shift over the years from quantification offered by psychometric intelligence testing based on a model of IQ constancy, to an in-depth individualized assessment based on the concept of chronic functional limitations to self-sufficiency.

The inadequacies of IQ testing in isolation may be similar to some of the diagnostic procedures applied to the chronically mentally ill. Perhaps researchers in the latter field will find that the kind of emphasis on functional assessment described above would be more productive than medical diagnosis in ascertaining the needs and appropriate services for individuals.

The Affective Life of the Disabled Person

The affective life of the individual is a significant dimension in research on the personal characteristics of the mentally retarded people that affect self-sufficiency. Initially, this area was ignored because of the focus upon IQ deficit alone. In a groundbreaking study, MacAndrew (1973) studied the interpersonal relationships of two profoundly mentally retarded people in a large institution. Through detailed observation of these two nonverbal adults, he identified their robust friendship. This study helped to promote an awareness among researchers that profoundly mentally retarded people could have friendships and that the affective life of the mentally retarded individual should be valued in the delivery of services promoting self sufficiency. Findings from subsequent ethnographic studies have provided additional support for the notion that being mentally retarded does not diminish the need for friendships in meeting the challenge of community living. In fact, friendships are in some ways predictive of successful community placements. Edgerton (1967) found that mentally retarded people who had left institutions were more successful in adapting to community life if they could make an informal relationship with a mentor in the community. Ability to engage another person in a caring relationship seemed to be an important determinant of self-sufficiency.

Edgerton's study was an ethnography of deinstitutionalized adult mentally retarded people; he used extensive interviews and observations to describe personal friendships, relationships, and other factors that affected their success in adjusting to community living. This methodology of ethnography and participant observation has recently been used by researchers who had worked with Edgerton—for example Berkovici (1933) and Dudley (1983), a social work researcher. Their goals have been to develop a fuller picture of the personal variables that correlated with self-sufficiency in the community, thus enabling subsequent researchers to pursue the identified issues in empirical studies. The 1983 presidential address to the American Association of Mental Deficiency (O'Connor, 1984) emphasized the importance of the friendships and social support networks of mentally retarded people. It was a call for researchers and practitioners to focus upon this issue.

Social Behavior

The recognition of the need for appropriate social behaviors has been heightened by the trend towards care in the community. The absence of appropriate social behaviors minimizes the likelihood of positive social encounters and is a main cause for failure of community placements. People with developmental disabilities are often not accepted because of bothersome, inappropriate, or antisocial behavior—bullying, fighting, showing off, swearing, lying, cheating, excessive or loud verbalizations, repetition, or an absence of positive social behaviors. People who have lived for extended periods in institutions often learn adaptive behaviors for that environment, which are nonproductive in the community environment. The development of a repertoire of interpersonal skills that enables one to interact successfully with other people has been recognized as critically important to self-sufficiency. Optimum adjustment and conformity in the community will only be obtained when social aspects of appropriate and acceptable social behaviors are promoted by the normalizing environment in which they reside (MacEachron, 1983).

Social skills training appears to be a valuable procedure to aid integration into the community. Typically, treatment incorporates instructions, modeling, performance feedback, role playing, and social reinforcement as part of the social skills training package. The effectiveness of such treatments has been established by controlled studies (Grinell & Lieberman, 1981).

Life Span of the Individual

A more recent trend in mental retardation research has been to identify critical periods in the lifespan of the individual with mental retardation and to explore the personal characteristics that facilitate the person's successful negotiations of these periods. Selzer (1985), for example, is studying the support-network needs of aging persons who have developmental disabilities. People with developmental disabilities of different ages seem, not surprisingly, to have varying constellations of service needs (Suelzle & Kennan, 1981).

THE CHARACTERISTICS OF THE CARERS AND SOCIAL CONTEXT

Because people with mental retardation are dependent on others for meeting many of their physical, social, and financial needs, the role of carers is critical to their functioning over the life span. Although the age of onset is much earlier for people with mental retardation than for people with mental illness, both populations are affected by the carers in their environment. Research on the family as carers and on professionals and staff as carers provides thought-provoking results for researchers in chronic mental illness.

Researchers have always recognized the importance of families in caring for mentally retarded people. One focus of the research has been on the relationships between the family, as the primary care-giver, and the relevant professionals. Two studies have examined ways to increase the effectiveness of this partnership.

The National Institute of Mental Health (NIMH) is currently funding a study on the "informing interview." Maynard (1986) is examining in detail the transcriptions of physicians informing patients of the diagnosis of their child's mental retardation. He has identified several characteristics of the interview process which lead to successful integration of the "bad news." One strategy is the matching by physicians of their vocabulary describing the child's developmental delay with the words used by the parents. By repeating the exact phrases, the physician can facilitate the assimilation of the diagnosis. Parental agreement with the diagnosis is a significant predictor of high compliance ratio of parents with professionals' recommendations (Wikler & Stoycheff, 1976). Thus the strategies explored by Maynard for aiding that agreement have many service implications.

In an effort to increase parent-professional partnership, a study was conducted in which parents of mentally retarded children were treated as consumers of social services and were asked to participate in giving feedback to social work students after observing them conduct interviews. As consumers who were currently not in crisis, the parents expressed their wishes to have social workers treat them as partners and to have social workers "really listen" to what parents say. In addition, they wanted social workers to be aware that parents cope effectively *most* of the time, and see social workers only when they are in crisis or in need of services. Students reported benefitting from this positive perspective on parents (Wikler, 1979).

Families are a current emphasis of federal research funding by NICHD and by the Administration of Developmental Disabilities of the Department of Health and Human Services. Specifically, there is a concern to determine the appropriate balance between family and professional input to maintain the mentally retarded person in the family home. In the last several years, 19 states have enacted legislation for family support in which cash subsidies or vouchers for services are made available to families identified as being at risk for placing their mentally retarded child outside of the home (Slater et al., 1986). Payments range from $160 per month to $680 per month, depending on the state; these costs contrast with the costs as high as $5,000 per month for institutionalization or $1500 per month for foster home care. Researchers are investigating the relative benefits of these types of programs. Issues include how to increase parents feeling of power, how to facilitate the parental role in case management, how to promote familial contacts with informal networks rather than increasing dependence on professionals, and how to identify and respond to the individual family's unique service needs.

One feature of chronically mentally ill persons is their disengagement from family support. Rather than studying the family as partners to professionals, studies seem to have focused more on the potentially negative effects of the family of the chronically mentally ill person. Studying ways to support the family's caring role may be a useful direction for researchers in the field of chronic mental illness (Wasow & Wikler, 1983).

Several factors that increase a family's ability to care successfully for a mentally retarded person have been identified in recent research reports. These include the impact of perceived stress associated with the presence of a retarded child, and the family's coping resources and support networks (Crnic, Fredrich & Greenberg, 1983). Support networks have been operationalized using measures of intimate social support, marital satisfaction, peer and friend availability, and extended family social support (Friedrich, Wilturner & Glen, 1985). Social supports are critical predictors of coping (Dunst, 1986). An additional focus of research has been the changes in family stress over the life span of the person with mental retardation (Suelzle and Keenan, 1981; Wikler, Wasow and Hatfield, 1981; Wikler, 1986). The types of intervention that might be effective in helping families cope with these stresses vary at different times (O'Hara, Chaiklin & Mosher, 1980). Table 1 lists stressors and the interventions that have proven helpful to families.

Similar stresses may characterize families of the chronically mentally ill. Research could identify particular stresses and evaluate the effectiveness of interventions over time.

Recently, there has been a focus on exploring strengths and coping strategies in these families. Families often report being stronger because of raising a child with mental retardation, but social service workers have underestimated the likelihood that parents would report such a gain (Wikler, Wasow & Hatfield, 1983). By primarily focusing on stresses rather than strengths, and on failures rather than coping, researchers and social workers may miss an important part of the picture.

Research on families of mentally retarded children has been influenced by family-stress theorists such as Hill and McCubbin. Their research delineates factors that can mediate the long-term impact of accumulated chronic and acute stressors on families. "Buffer" variables include the family's perception of the stressor (i.e., the mental retardation); the family's coping strategies, resilience, and adaptability; and access to support networks (including informal and formal supports). Each of these has been studied separately as variables, as well as in combination. Recent work by Dunst (1986) and Nihira, Mink, and Meyers (1984) explore these issues, and support the models indicating directions for service provision that strengthens the family in its effort to maintain the mentally retarded person as a member of the family.

Studies on effective strategies for helping families to care for their mentally retarded member (Rose, 1976; Intagliata, 1984; Schilling, 1983) have emphasized parent groups as an approach for disseminating knowledge and building skills. There has been an assumption that parents can often help one another in ways that professionals cannot. Moroney (1979) contrasts the attitudes shown in professional, clinical, and research studies on

Table 1

Stressors and Interventions to Help Families

Stressors	Effective Interventions
Need for information on caring for a mentally retarded person	Training manuals; autobiographies by parents; access to specialists and clinics; information at critical junctures; access to other parents; support groups
Grieving/guilt/helplessness/chronic sorrow	Active listening by family and friends; contact with other parents to normalize the experience; supportive counseling; anticipatory guidance over the life span
Burden of care and extraordinary work for extended periods without interruption	In-home respite care provided by family, friends, neighbors, trained volunteers, professionals; contact with other parents to normalize the experience; assertiveness training; money for extra care-giver supports; money for transportation
Stigmatized interactions with society	Access to parent groups for support and for sharing of successful strategies; assertiveness training; attitudinal changes in society
Financial strain	Access to extra sources of monetary support—Medicaid, Supplemental Security Income, family support funds
Social isolation	Respite care; parent organizations with outreach; extended family involvement in clinic programs; promotion of neighborhood projects and church projects; parent groups
Chronic stresses and periodic stresses over time	Case management over life span
Unique strains of each mentally retarded person and each family	Menu of services available to families rather than one package deal

parents of severely mentally retarded people with those on parents of chronically mentally ill people. He points out that parents of people with chronic mental illness are often considered to be a part of the problem, while parents of the mentally retarded are treated as partners with the professionals, working together to maximize the functioning of the disabled person. As long as researchers perceive parents as being part of the problem, it is unlikely that the effectiveness of parent groups will be studied.

Stability and continuity in the mentally retarded person's environment are characteristics of carers that contribute to self-sufficiency. An unfortunate feature of community care has been the high turnover of staff, resulting in part from low pay, inadequate training, and an isolated work setting. Researchers have identified factors in some programs that have overcome the problem of high staff turnover. Those factors—training in behavioral management (Schinke, 1977), peer support groups, and respite care for the staff—are broadly the same as those identified as supportive of families (with the exception of grief counseling). It is possible that such factors could also be of significance for the carers of people with chronic mental illness.

INTERACTIONS BETWEEN PERSON AND CARER CHARACTERISTICS

Recent research has shown that neither the personal characteristics nor the carer characteristics is alone predictive of self-sufficiency. The fit between the two is significant. The basic social work concept of the person in the situation is central to both assessment and interventions of a population struggling with chronic dependency. Several studies illustrate this point.

In the assessment of mental handicap, the work of Caldwell et al. (1979) developed a tool to measure the interaction and fit of a preschool child's home environment and the mother's interactive style with the child's level of functioning. She found this tool to be a better predictor of IQ in longitudinal studies than the traditionally used tests that focused on the child alone.

The New York Longitudinal Study (Thomas & Chess, 1984) identified temperamental characteristics of infants, and followed over 200 subjects from birth through the early twenties. The recent reports assessed psychopathology of young adults and correlated it with temperamental and familial data collected over the years. Certain clusters of features in infants put them at increased risk for adult disorders. In addition, Thomas and Chess emphasized in their discussion that the interaction of the environment with the children at risk—the fit—may ultimately determine the level of adult mental health functioning.

Child-development researchers are currently searching for behavioral coding systems which can capture what is referred to as reciprocity, or mutuality. The focus of their studies is on the extent to which the interactive dyad is capable of reading one another's cues and responding to them accordingly, rather than letting one member of the dyad (usually the adult) dominate the rhythm and the topic of the interaction. The assumption that is increasingly gaining support from empirical studies is that this fit between partners is more predictive of eventual competence than specific styles of behavior of either partner.

Numerous studies have been conducted on the interactive styles of parents with their mentally retarded children, comparing it with that of parents of normal children. The dominant finding has been that the former are more directive and protective than the latter (Brody & Stoneman, 1983). These findings do not imply that mental handicap could be avoided by increasing the environmental responsiveness towards the mentally retarded individual, but it suggests that the self-perception, level of achievement, and range of self-sufficiency in adult life would be affected by these variables.

Dunst (1986) surveyed a group of parents and assessed the relationship between social supports of the parents and parental overprotection of the mentally retarded child. He reported that they were inversely correlated: the more socially isolated the parents, the more overprotective they were with their child; the more connected they were to their environment, the more responsive they were to the child. Wikler, Stevenson, and Seitz (1983) reported on a project in which they trained parents of mentally retarded children to be less directive and more responsive to their child's initiations in a free play setting. Using an experimental design, they presented videotapes before and after training of the parents, along with videotapes of a parent of a normal child of the same maturational age to five groups of students (n = 94). The students reported liking the mentally retarded child whose parent had been trained to be responsive more than the child of the untrained parent; they also liked the mentally retarded child as much as they liked the normal child. The discussion suggested that the fit in the mother-child dyad affected the lay observers' perceptions of the child with the handicap.

Zetlin and Turner (1984) conducted extensive exploratory interviews of 46 adults with mental retardation in the community, and their parents. They showed that acceptance of one's handicap seemed related (1) to lack of overprotectiveness by the parents and (2) to increased self-sufficiency in the community as adults. The history of a good fit between the child with mental retardation and his environment may ultimately relate to increased competence in functioning in the community.

Dudley (1983) conducted an ethnographic study documenting the lives of 27 people who were labelled mentally retarded (22 were mildly mentally retarded and five were considered moderately retarded) who live in a major Eastern city. He took extensive field notes from observations made over an eleven-month period, in which he interacted with them in their homes, restaurants, work sites, social gatherings, and agency-sponsored events. The field research focused on their social world and how an invisible wall of social stigma continues to segregate this population. He identified their circumstances in detail and provided examples of well-meaning staff who inadvertently promote stigmatizing experiences for these people. He concluded by suggesting a range of recommendations that, if followed, could enhance the integration of mentally retarded people into the community.

These studies represent several distinct methodologies, each of which begins to address the issue of interaction between the person and the situation. Researchers in the field of chronic mental illness could also conduct studies of the kind described above to determine how likeability, social supports, and interactive fit could be enhanced. The outcomes of such research might change the approaches of families, staff, and program policies so that chronically mentally ill people could be more acceptable to the broader community and more able to be self-sufficient.

SUPPORT GROUPS

In the field of mental retardation there have been concerted efforts from at least two groups of carers to promote exemplary services. The National Association of Retarded Citizens, founded in 1950, has provided an inestimable source of peer support for parents, as well as lobbying on behalf of mentally retarded people for legislation, research, and funding of programs promoting the rights of people with mental retardation. This kind of energy and enthusiasm has been taken up more recently by the National Alliance for the Mentally Ill.

In the early 1970s, the relevant professional and parent organizations worked together to establish an accrediting body, the Accreditation Council on Mental Retardation and Developmental Disabilities (ACMRDD), for services to the mentally retarded. The council developed a set of standards for institutional and community-based programs that protects the rights and interests of the mentally retarded and insures the quality of services provided by carers. These standards are revised regularly to reflect state-of-the-art research and professional practices as well as to provide an educative framework for carers in the community.

CONCLUSION

This has been a selective review of the research on dependency and self-sufficiency among people with developmental disabilities. Researchers in the field of chronic mental illness may be able to use some of the studies described to advance their work in assessing and maximizing the individual's skills in community living, on supporting professionals and families in their caring role, and on the design of services.

REFERENCES

American Association on Mental Deficiency. (1974). Adaptive behavior scale for children and adults. Washington, D.C.

Begab, M., Haywood, H., & Garber, H. (Eds.) (1981).*Psychosocial influences in retarded performance.* Baltimore: University Park Press.

Bercovici, S. (1983). *Barriers to normalization: The restrictive management of retarded persons.* Baltimore: University Park Press.

Caldwell, B. & Bradley, R. (1979). *Home observation for measurement of the environment.* Little Rock: University of Arkansas.

Crnic, K., Friedrich, W., & Greenberg, N. (1983). Adaptation of families with mentally retarded children: A model of stress, coping and family ecology. *American Journal of Mental Deficiency, 88*(2), 125-138.

Dudley, J. *Living with stigma.* Springfield, IL: Charles C. Thomas.

Dunst, C., Trivette, C., & Cross, A. (1986). Mediating influences of social support: Personal, family, and child outcomes. *American Journal of Mental Deficiency, 90*(4), 403-417.

Dybwad, G. & Cherington, D. (Eds.) (1980). *New neighbors: The retarded citizen in quest of a home.* Washington, D.C.: U.S. Department of Health and Human Services. President's Committee on Mental Retardation. OHDS Publication No. 80-21004.

Edgerton, R. (1967). *The cloak of competence: Stigma in the lives of the mentally retarded.* Berkeley: University of California Press.

Edgerton, R. (1983). Failure in community adaption: The relativity of assessment. In K. Kerman, M. Begab, & R. Edgerton (Eds.), *Environments and behaviour. The adaption of mentally retarded persons.* Baltimore: University Park Press.

Edgerton, R., Bollinger, M., & Herr, B. (1984). The cloak of competence: After two decades. *American Journal of Mental Deficiency, 88*(4), 345-351.

Edgerton, R. (Ed.) (1984). *Lives in process: Mildly retarded adults in a large city.* Washington, D.C.: American Association on Mental Deficiency, Monograph #6.

Eheart, B. (1982). Mother, child interactions with non-retarded and mentally retarded preschoolers. *American Journal of Mental Deficiency, 87*(1), 20-25.

Friedrich, W., Wilturner, L., & Cohen, D. (1985). Coping resources and parenting mentally retarded children. *American Journal of Mental Deficiency, 90*(2), 130-139.

Grinnell, R. & Lieberman, A. (1981). Helping mentally retarded persons get jobs. In S.P. Schinke (Ed.), *Behavioral methods in social welfare.* New York: Aldine Publishing Co.

Hill, R. (1958). Generic features of families under stress. *Social Casework, 39,* 3-9.

Kaufman, S. (1984). Friendship, coping systems and community adjustment of mentally retarded adults. In R.B. Edgerton (Ed.), *Lives in process: Mildly retarded adults in a large city.* Washington, D.C.: American Association on Mental Deficiency, Monograph #6.

McAndrew, C. & Edgerton, R. (1984). On the possibility of friendship. *American Journal of Mental Deficiency, 70,* 25-30.

MacEachron, A. (1983). Institutional reform and adaptive functioning of mentally retarded persons: A field experiment. *American Journal of Mental Deficiency, 88*(1), 2-12.

McCubbin, H. & Patterson, J. (1983). Family stress adaption to crises: A double ABCX model of family behavior. In H. McCubbin, M. Sussman, and J. Patterson (Eds.), *Social stresses and the family: Advances and developments in family stress theory and research.* New York: The Haworth Press.

McDonald-Wikler, L. (1986, in press). Periodic stresses in families of older mentally retarded children: An exploratory study.

McDonald-Wikler, L., Stevenson, M., & Seitz, S. (1983). Lay observers' perceptions of mental retardation as affected by responsiveness of mothers. Paper presented to American Association on Mental Deficiency National Convention, Houston, Texas.

Menolascino, F. & McCann, B. (1983). *Mental health and mental retardation: Bridging the gap.* Baltimore: University Park Press.

Mink, I., Meyers, C., & Nihira, K. (1984). Taxonomy of family life styles: II. Homes with slow-learning children. *American Journal of Mental Deficiency, 89*(2), 111-123.

Moroney, R. (1980). *Families, social services, and social policy: The issue of shared responsibility.* Rockville, Maryland: National Institute of Mental Health, DHSS Publication No. (ADM) 80-846.

Nihira, K., Foster, R., Shellhaas, M., & Leland, H. (1974). *AAMD Adaptive Behaviour Scale.* Washington, D.C.: American Association on Mental Deficiency.

Nihira, K., Meyers, C., & Mink, I. (1983). Home environment, family adjustment and the development of mentally retarded children. *Applied Research in Mental Retardation, 1,* 5-24.

O'Connor, G. (1983). Social support for mentally retarded persons. *Mental Retardation, 21*(5), 187-196.

O'Hara, D., Chaiklin, H., & Mosher, B. (1980). A family life-cycle plan for delivering services to the developmentally handicapped. *Child Welfare, 59*(2), 80-90.

Peterson, P. (1981). Stressors, outcome dysfunction, and resources in mothers of children with handicaps. Lincoln, Nebraska: University of Nebraska, unpublished dissertation.

Romer, D. & Berkson, G. (1981). Social ecology of supervised community facilities for mentally disabled adults: II. Predictors of affiliation. *American Journal of Mental Deficiency, 85*(3), 229-242.

Rose, S. (1974). Training parents in groups as behaviour modifiers of their mentally retarded children. *Journal of Behaviour Therapy and Experimental Psychiatry, 5,* 135-140.

Schilling, R., Gilchrist, L., & Schinke, S. (1984). Coping and social support in families of developmentally disabled children. *Family Relations, 33,* 47-54.

Schinke, S. & Wong, S. (1977). Evaluation of staff training in group homes for retarded persons. *American Journal of Mental Deficiency, 3,* 130-137.

Selzer, M. (1985). Informal supports for aging mentally retarded persons. *American Journal of Mental Deficiency, 90*(3), 259-265.

Slater, M., Bates, M., Eicher, L., & Wikler, L. (1986). Survey: statewide family support programs. *Applied Research in Mental Retardation, 7,* 241-257.

Stoneman, Z., Brody, C., & Abbott, D. (1983). In-house observations of young down syndrome children with their mothers and fathers. *American Journal of Mental deficiency, 87,* 591-600.

Suelzle, M. & Keenan, V. (1981). Changes in family support networks over the life cycle of mentally retarded persons. *American Journal of Mental Deficiency, 86,* 267-274.

Thomas, H. & Chess, S. (1984). Genesis and evolution of behavioral disorders: From infancy to early adult life. *American Journal of Psychiatry, 141,* 1-9.

Wasow, M. & Wikler, L. (1983). Reflections on professionals' attitudes toward the severely mentally retarded and the chronically mentally ill: Implications for parents. *Family Therapy, 10*(3), 299-308.

Wikler, L. (1979). Consumer involvement in training of social work students. *Social Casework, 60*(3), 145-149.

Wikler, L., Wasow, M., & Hatfield, A. (1983). Seeking strengths in families of developmentally disabled children. *Social Work, 28*(4), 313-315.

Zetlin, A. & Turner, J. (1984). Self-perspectives on being handicapped: Stigma and adjustment. In R.B. Edgerton (Ed.), *Lives in process: Mildly retarded adults in a large city.* Washington, D.C.: American Association on Mental Deficiency, Monograph #6, 121-144.

PART II: RESEARCH DESIGN

Introduction

Allen Rubin

One of the hardest problems researchers face, one which can temporarily immobilize even experienced researchers, is how to make a study feasible without sacrificing methodological rigor or inferential capacity. The literature on mental health program evaluation is replete with outcome studies based on incomplete designs that failed to control for threats to internal validity. Were investigators simply unaware of rigorous design alternatives that would have controlled for those threats?

This question can be answered by anyone who has attempted to conduct rigorous, true experimental studies in an agency setting. It is easy to conceive of a true experiment, but try to convince an agency to let you implement it. Consider, for example, an agency's likely response to a plan for random assignment of clients to experimental versus control (denial of service?) conditions, and for measurement of those clients by raters who are not working with them and who are blind as to their treatment condition. Consider further that one may not only have to persuade an agency administrator to allow the research, but also the agency's board members and practitioners. On top of that, there is the problem of human subjects review and informed consent, perhaps requiring that clients agree to random assignment to a no-service condition.

If research on chronic mental illness were done only under ideal methodological conditions, mental health journals would be a lot thinner. However, even under the ideal research condi-

113

tions, no single study "proves" anything. Even the best studies are open to question. For example, random assignment does not guarantee that the control and experimental groups will be really equivalent; it only offers a high mathematical probability that they will be. Every study has attributes that can be questioned on methodological or inferential grounds. It follows, then, that the design of research does not require eliminating every conceivable source of doubt, but rather removing as many as possible within one's feasibility constraints. That done, the researcher must then ask if the resultant design is still worth doing—that is, despite its flaws, if the study will add enough to the knowledge-building enterprise to warrant the effort and resources required.

In answering this question, one must keep in mind the potential heuristic value of a study as well as the role of replication. For example, if a simple pre-test/post-test pilot study yields extreme findings in an area never before studied and therefore spawns a host of more controlled studies, the original study would have been well worth doing despite its methodological or inferential limitations. Suppose, for example, that a simple pre-test/post-test study of social work student attitudes about chronic mental illness found surprising evidence that after two years of MSW education those attitudes were more negative about the mentally ill than before that education. Although there may be several rival hypotheses as to why students' attitudes did not improve or why change has occurred in an undesired direction, the field benefits from learning—on descriptive grounds alone—that this phenomenon is occurring. Further research might then attempt to sort out which rival hypotheses really explain this phenomenon.

The papers in Part II discuss some of the methodologies that researchers in this field have been applying to important research questions. These chapters illustrate that there are excellent alternatives to true experimental research in trying to investigate these questions. Sriniki Jayaratne's paper, chapter 6, discusses the utility of time-series and single-subject designs. These designs can offer a credible degree of internal validity, and through replication can build generalizable findings. Equally important, single-subject designs provide a way to deal with the difficult problem of diversity among the population suffering from chronic mental illness. Group experiments typically include a heterogeneous sample from this population. Since outcome results are never uniform across all patients, even the best group experiments do not guarantee that their aggregate results will apply to any single future patient. Single-subject designs provide one way for clinicians to assess applicability to specific patients and for researchers to begin to sort out what specific methods of intervention produce what specific outcomes with what specific types of chronic patients.

In chapter 7, Claudia Coulton addresses the problem of patient diversity. Her work offers a methodological approach for assessing specific types of residential environments for specific types of chronic patients. Person-environment fit is a concept much in vogue these days in the social work literature; Coulton's paper offers a way to operationalize it. The next two chapters, by Steven Segal and Phyllis Solomon, deal with longitudinal designs. Solomon's paper uses an example from her own research to illustrate the utility of these designs and their advantages and disadvantages. Segal focuses on the practical difficulties associated with implementing longitudinal research in the study of chronic mental illness—particularly regarding the tracking of patients—and how his research dealt with these difficulties.

Part II does not address all of the important methodologies applicable to research on the chronically mentally ill. As is the case in any conference, not everyone doing important research in this field was able to participate in the conference upon which this book is based or to submit publishable papers. Two methodologies that are not included in this volume are particularly noteworthy because of the important studies on chronic mental illness that have applied them. One such omission is research that utilizes primarily qualitative methods that probe deeply into the subjective meanings of phenomena to those affected by them. These methods rely heavily on symbolic-interaction theory, focus more on the generation or empirical grounding of theory and hypotheses than on their verification, and are likely to use participant observation or ethnographic data-gathering techniques. An important recent study applying qualitative methods was an ethnographic study of the homeless mentally ill in three eastern cities, conducted by Baxter and Hopper (1982). Their main data collection method was participant observation, which meant at times posing as homeless themselves. Their findings documented the inhumane conditions in public shelters for the homeless and questioned prevailing beliefs that when the homeless refuse shelter it is because of their impaired judgment. By qualitatively delving into the subjective meaning of the phenomenon of homelessness, Baxter and Hopper concluded that "the decision by many homeless people to fend for themselves on the streets gains a measure of rationality and intelligibility" due to the inhumane conditions in the shelters.

Another omission from this section is research that utilizes multivariate statistical procedures to offset some of the threats to internal validity associated with an inability to implement a randomized experimental design. This approach tries to measure as many extraneous variables as possible that would have been controlled through random assignment and then to control for those variables in a multivariate statistical analysis, such as multiple regression analysis or discriminant function analysis. These approaches enable the researcher, on statistical grounds, to partition out how much of the variation in the dependent variable (client outcome) is attributable to the independent variable (treatment condition) when extraneous potential differences between experimental and comparison groups are held constant. If the researcher has assessed all of the extraneous variables that readers can conceive of as likely rival explanations of experimental- and comparison-group outcome differences, and if the effect of the treatment condition upon outcome is substantial after all those extraneous variables have been statistically controlled for, then inferences that treatment is effective have sufficient plausibility to guide service delivery decision making for the time being. True, randomized experimental research might be a preferable test of treatment efficacy, but when such research is infeasible, studies utilizing adequate multivariate statistical controls may be worth doing.

One important study on chronic mental illness that illustrates this methodology was conducted by Nuehring et al. (1980). It utilized discriminant function analysis to identify the background, situational, client-attribute, or service delivery variables that best predicted state mental rehospitalization. The strongest predictor of readmission was a patient's relation to outpatient aftercare, with those continuing in aftercare more likely to be readmitted.

A similar study—also using discriminant function analysis to differentiate state hospital readmissions from nonreadmissions—was conducted by Solomon et al. (1984). It controlled statistically for a wide range of demographic variables (age, living arrangements, etc.) and clinical variables (diagnosis, degree of chronicity and treatments received during hospitalization). Like the work of Nuehring et al., Solomon and her colleagues sought to isolate the impact of utilizing aftercare services on readmission. They found that the most significant predictor of readmission was the variety of aftercare services utilized and the extent to which those services were the ones that social workers assessed the patients as needing. Solomon et al. concluded that the Nuehring study had different results because it did not control for the variety and relevance of the aftercare services utilized. A comparison of these two studies illustrates both the value and the risks of relying on multivariate statistical controls.

REFERENCES

Baxter, E. & Hopper, K. (1982). The new mendicancy: Homeless in New York City. *American Journal of Orthopsychiatry, 52*(3), 393-407.

Neuhring, E., Thayer, J., & Lander, R. (1980). On the factors predicting rehospitalization among two state mental hospital populations. *Administration in Mental Health, 7,* 247-270.

Solomon, P., Gordon, B., & Davis, J. (1984). Differentiating psychiatric readmissions from nonreadmissions. *American Journal of Orthopsychiatry, 34*(3), 426-435.

Chapter 6
The Use of Time-Series Designs in Research with the Chronically Mentally Ill

Sirinika Jayaratne

Six years ago, a report to the Secretary of the Department of Health and Human Services, *Toward a National Plan for the Chronically Mentally Ill* (1980), summarized several research and evaluation goals for researchers studying the problems and treatment of chronic patients. One of the identified goals was an understanding of the relationship between delivery of treatment and its outcome. The *National Plan* called upon researchers to delineate which services benefit which clients. This theme has been stated and restated by clinical researchers in the intervening years.

This paper discusses the single-subject, or time-series, design—a research model that is particularly suited to address this question. The terms *single-subject* and *time-series* are used synonymously in this paper to mean any research strategy that employs multiple measurement points and the introduction of an intervention that divides the data into segments of baseline and treatment (Bloom & Fisher, 1982; Campbell & Stanley, 1963; Hersen & Barlow, 1976; Jayaratne & Levy, 1979). The contention that the time-series design is a useful method of inquiry on this issue is based on four assumptions about services to the chronically mentally ill.

First, it assumes that there is still much to learn about the goodness-of-fit between the method of treatment and desired client outcomes. Few of the strategies used with the chronically mentally ill in prior research efforts appear to have addressed this question adequately. Many prior research efforts employed either group designs or large-scale descriptive surveys, neither of which can address the question of goodness-of-fit at the level of the individual client.

Second, chronic patients will respond best when the changes sought and the intervention procedures used are well defined (Paul & Lentz, 1977). That is, specification of both the *methods* of change and the *outcomes* of change efforts is not simply a desired end result—it is a necessary research and clinical endeavor because it directly affects how treatment is conducted. While this assumption is made within the context of clinical desirability, it is a necessary requirement in implementing a good research strategy.

Third, the development of adaptive social skills and the suppression of maladaptive behaviors must be continuously fostered and nurtured through various supportive arrangements (Paul, Tobia & Holly, 1972; Fairweather, Sanders & Cressly, 1969; Tessler & Goldman, 1982). Thus service delivery may have to be extensive and maintained for a long time. Measures that rely on an absolute event, such as rehospitalization, do not provide the quality of data that tap the diversity and trends in client behavior. The effects of various supportive arrangements can be examined only by employing time-series measures.

Finally, among the various possible outcome measures, the dimensions of psychosocial functioning and vocational competence are of primary importance (Pepper & Ryglewicz, 1984). These factors have been identified because they have been recognized in the literature as closely associated with the individual's quality of life. To date, however, the predominant measures of treatment effectiveness have been symptom remission and relapse (*National Plan,* 1980). These measures are necessary but not sufficient measures of outcome, because they tend to be somewhat global and terminal in nature and provide little data on the immediate effects of treatment. For a data collection strategy to be valuable for treatment, it must provide ongoing information on behavioral and affective change in the client's life.

To the extent that these four assumptions are valid, the use of time-series, or single-subject, designs seems almost a natural selection. In fact, the origins of this research strategy lie in the study of the chronically mentally ill population. Single-subject methodology had its clinical birth nearly two decades ago in mental institutions with patients who could best be described as chronic (Atthowe & Krasner, 1968; Ayllon, 1965; Schaefer & Martin, 1966). These studies had a major impact on the development of interventions with this population. The proposed time-series research strategy is, therefore, not a radical one but rather an argument for a "back-to-basics" approach. In proposing this design, the suggestion is neither that alternative research strategies be discarded nor that single-subject or time-series designs alone are sufficient. What is being suggested is that this methodology offers a promising point of entry to the question of the best fit between a method of treatment and a patient.

THE FIT OF DESIGN TO THE PROBLEM

The natural fit between time-series designs and chronic mental illness can be seen by comparing key features of this research strategy to the nature of chronic mental illness:

- The time-series design, as its name suggests, measures problems and goals over time. Chronicity, by definition, involves problems of long duration with multiple episodes. The structure of the time-series design appears to have a clear relationship to the topography of chronic mental illness.
- Because measurement is continuous in a time-series design, both the amount of behavioral change and the conditions surrounding the change are more recognizable. That is, changes in behavior and related data patterns become more apparent by virtue of measurement continuity. Because most chronic patients do not show symptoms continuously, and because they may be seen by professionals only in times of crisis, this strategy of data collection helps to identify factors surrounding both the "good times" and the "bad times."

- Time-series designs identify a beginning point of intervention, which produces an environment in which the service provider is forced to identify the components of a change effort and to relate the change effort to specific changes in behaviors or sets of behaviors and affect. Since the design is idiographic, the relationship between change efforts and actual change can be drawn more easily than with a group design or survey. The resulting specification enhances both the potential for replication and knowledge transfer. As the *National Plan* points out, "for specific applications of psychosocial treatments to gain acceptance, they must not only be effective, they must also be replicable by people other than the originators of the treatment" (pp. 2-104).
- Time-series designs require the specification of outcomes in discrete, measurable terms. The presence of maladaptive behaviors and the development of appropriate social skills refer to discrete events which, for the most part, can be operationalized in measurable terms. The measurement tactics of time-series designs coincide with the current needs of researchers who study the chronically mentally ill. As Pepper and Rygiewicz (1984) point out, "treatment directed toward the development of self-awareness, coping skills, and affective behavior, and goal directed activity... (that is, treatment) that attend to the here-and-now of functioning" (p. 4) is what needs to be addressed.
- Because of problems typically associated with gathering data from chronic patients, researchers have turned to the service providers and agency records (and sometimes the family) for information. This tactic is not precluded by time-series designs, but the focus on discrete behaviors makes the process more amenable to direct client involvement, thereby increasing opportunities for measurement triangulation and, possibly, clinical efficacy.

SOME ILLUSTRATIVE EXAMPLES

As noted earlier, there is a significant body of literature on the use of time-series methodology within institutional settings that demonstrates the utility and efficacy of this research model with chronically mentally ill patients. On the other hand, reports on the use of time-series designs with the outpatient chronically mentally ill appear infrequently in the literature. One major factor accounting for this lack of reporting could be that researchers in this area tend to focus on specific behaviors and pay little attention to diagnostic categories and labels. In other words, the term "chronic mental illness" and its subsidiary diagnoses play a minimal role in the measurement of clinical change. Another plausible reason is the lack of control over the environment in which clinical research is being conducted. Clinician-researchers who possess these data may not view them as publishable research studies per se; instead, they may simply see them as examples of good clinical practice. In addition, there could be a myriad of reasons, ranging from inadequate funding for this type of research to conceptual concerns about the generalizability of data.

Two ongoing cases are presented below. The purpose is not to evaluate the quality, value, or success of the treatment programs in question, but simply to consider the dimensions related to the use of time-series designs in these instances.

Case Study 1

This case involves a 32-year old unemployed married male, who was referred to a family service agency by a community mental health center. The case was referred because the man's wife was concerned about the "health" of the marriage. This man has been diagnosed as paranoid schizophrenic interspersed with manic-depressive episodes. Lithium has been prescribed, but he refuses to take it. His hospitalization has been cyclical, with his wife admitting him to the hospital each spring for the last five years or so.

During the course of interviews, the worker collected verbal response patterns, with the goal of making the patient's verbal behavior more appropriate. For example, when the worker asked a question, "How are you feeling today?," the patient responded, "The bluebirds are flying in the sky." In this instance, the targeted behavior is directly observed and measured during the course of treatment.

Following the therapist's instigation, data were collected by both the patient and his wife at home. The targeted behaviors are very specific, and change goals are being pursued in small steps. The targeted behavior occurrence or nonoccurrence was monitored by both husband and wife, thereby corroborating or validating each other's observations. The assumption, of course, is that the data gathered are central and related to the problem of remission and rehospitalization.

The important point here is the demonstration of patient involvement in the data-gathering process, with accuracy being reported upon by the spouse. Self-monitoring is reasonably reliable because the outcome variables are specific, tangible events. The use of more global outcome measures, such as a set of paper-and-pencil measures, might not have produced any fruitful data from this patient.

Case Study 2

This case involves a single 31-year old female on welfare. While one could question whether this particular case fits the definition of chronically mentally ill, it does involve a patient who has had multiple hospitalizations. Since about age 14, she has been diagnosed as being depressed. She reports that she has a poor memory, occasionally thinks of suicide (although she has never attempted it), has high blood pressure, and is an insomniac. She has been hospitalized several times for both depression and substance abuse, usually as a result of a massive intake of alcohol or marijuana. She has been prescribed a wide array of medication, most of which she refuses to take because she claims that it effects her coordination. She is an avid softball player, and reports that the medication adversely affects her play. She also reports that she smokes as many as 15 joints a day.

In all instances, the data are self-report data. One could, of course, argue about the accuracy of these data. What is clear, however, is that she is not afraid to report noncompliance with medication, nor is she afraid to report how much pot she smokes. This patient is not only capable of monitoring her own behavior, but she seems to be doing an extraordinary job. In effect, the design and measurement strategy has gotten the patient involved in treatment.

These two cases demonstrate both the feasibility and desirability of utilizing single-subject, or time-series designs, with the chronically mentally ill. The cases illustrate the usefulness of these designs in tracking those behavior patterns (which may be missed by averaging data) that in the long run may lead to rehospitalization. For example, case study 2 reveals that there was no change in the specific set of behaviors that had resulted in the patient being hospitalized previously. On the other hand, the patient claims that she is not depressed because she is participating in an activity she enjoys— as a result, the perceived need for medication is reduced, at least in the patient's mind. This raises questions about alternatives to medication as well as, in this instance, periodicity of drug intake.

Time-series designs specify treatment methods. In all instances, there is a defined point at which treatment is said to have begun, and this is the point at which an identifiable treatment program has been instituted. To the extent that these treatment programs are successful, this specification of the method of intervention facilitates their transferability and replicability.

CONCLUSION

There is a natural fit between the requirements of the time-series design and the nature of chronic mental illness. Yet the design configuration is only a beginning, not a solution, to the examination of the client-treatment-outcome triad. The design does not provide answers for every case. It may be difficult to discover the dynamics in a successful case. Clearly, we may need to take a step backward and return to the fundamentals. Turning at this time to more sophisticated designs (that would control external validity) such as control-group designs may be an overzealous endeavor in attempting to do too much too soon. Such programs may yield some general information about the relative utility of various treatment strategies; typically, however, they yield very little information about the best fit between the individual client and a specific treatment program (Hersen & Barlow, 1976; Jayaratne, 1977). For example, consider the large-scale evaluation of the Community Support Programs conducted by Tessler and Goldman (1982). In this study, in which data were collected primarily from service providers, the authors report that "for a significant minority of clients, social and leisure time is not productively filled" (p. 103). We know very little about what these individuals did, what they have done, or even why this was the case. Time-series designs and replication procedures could have generated clinically valuable information.

In contrast, note that the more recently published time-series studies with the chronically mentally ill have employed more sophisticated single-subject designs in outpatient settings. For example, Holmes, Hansen, and Lawrence (1984) taught conversational skills to ten chronic patients using a multiple baseline design to monitor clinical progress. Similarly, Kelly et al. (1979) used a multiple baseline design to teach job interviewing skills, and Hersen and Bellack (1976) also used a multiple baseline design to teach social skills to two chronic male schizophrenics.

In all of these studies, the outcomes were not only directly related to patient chronicity but were also specifically defined. Furthermore, in all instances the interventions employed were clearly defined, and in some instances program changes brought about by patient idiosyncracy were also articulated. This type of specification lays the groundwork for replication and generalizability.

External validity and generalizability have been perennial problems in time-series research. No doubt, a "true" sample would reflect a population better than a single individual. By the same token, significant inroads have been made in this regard, as is illustrated by developments in clinical and systematic replication (Hersen & Barlow, 1976; Thomas, 1984), meta-analyses and meta-analytic analogs (Gingerich, 1983; Jacobson,

Follette & Revenstorff, 1984), and generalizability theory, or G-theory (Cronbach, Glesser, Nanda & Rajaratnam, 1979; Strossen, Coates & Thoresen, 1979).

The obverse of this situation, of course, is the tendency to generalize from the group to the individual simply because the individual is part of the group. It is simply invalid to generalize from the group to the individual when the individual is idiosyncratic on some key variables. Such cases require information about the target person on dimensions of importance to the independent variable. If such data are absent or are ill-defined, individual differences tend to get lost within the group. Unfortunately, research with the chronically mentally ill appears to have paid greater attention to differences between groups than to differences within groups.

A strategy which utilizes the best of both worlds may be the method of choice. There is no reason, for example, why group designs cannot employ nested procedures (Kirk, 1968), whereby time-series data are collected on random subsamples of group members, and a clear effort is made to identify treatment procedures. Or, in surveys with chronic patients or their service providers, there is no reason why subsamples cannot be interviewed periodically (as opposed to a simple cross-sectional survey), thereby collecting frequent data which can then be fitted into a time-series framework for purposes of analysis. Time-series designs have much to offer in the delineation of what treatment best fits which client, and this methodology deserves a prominent place in research with chronically ill mental patients.

REFERENCES

Atthowe, J.M. & Krasner, L. (1968). Preliminary report on the application of contigent reinforcement procedures (token economy) on a chronic psychiatric ward. *Journal of Abnormal Psychology, 73,* 37-43.

Ayllon, T. (1965). Some behavioral problems associated with eating in chronic schizophrenic patients. In P. Ullmann & L. Krasner (Eds.), *Case studies in behavior modification.* New York: Holt, Rinehart & Winston.

Bloom, M. & Fisher, J. (1982). *Evaluating practice: Guidelines for the accountable professional.* Englewood Cliffs, N.J.: Prentice-Hall.

Campbell, D.T. & Stanley, J.C. (1963). *Experimental and quasi-experimental designs for research.* Chicago: Rand McNally.

Cronbach, L.J., Giesser, G.C., Nanda, H., & Rajanatnam, N. (1963). Theory of generalizability: A liberalization of reliability theory. *British Journal of Statistical Psychology, 16,* 13.

Fairweather, G., Saunders, D., Maynard, H., & Cressly, D. (1969). *Community life for the mentally ill: An alternative to institutional care.* Chicago: Aldine Publishing Company.

Gingerich, W.J. (1983). Meta-analysis of applied time-series data. *The Journal of Applied Behavioral Science, 20,* 71-79.

Hersen, M. & Bellack, A.S. (1976). A multiple baseline analysis of social skills training with chronic schizophrenics. *Journal of Applied Behavioral Analysis, 9,* 239-245.

Hersen, M. & Barlow, D.H. (1976). *Single-case experimental designs.* New York: Pergamon Press.

Holmes, M.R., Hansen, D.J., & St. Lawrence, J.S. (1984). Conversation skills training with aftercare patients in the community: Social validation and generalizability. *Behavior Therapy, 15,* 84-100.

Jacobson, N.S., Follette, W.C., & Revenstorff, D. (1984). Psychotherapy outcome research: Methods for reporting variability and evaluating clinical significance. *Behavior Therapy, 15,*336-352.

Jayaratne, S. (1977). Single-subject and group designs in treatment evaluation. *Social Work Research and Abstracts, 13,* 35-43.

Jayaratne, S. & Levy, R.L. (1979). *Empricial clinical practice.* New York: Columbia University Press.

Kelly, J.A., Laughlin, C., Clairborne, D., & Patterson, M.A. (1979). Group procedure for teaching job interviewing skills to formerly hospitalized patients. *Behavior therapy, 10,* 299-310.

Kirk, R.E. (1968). *Experimental design: Procedures for the behavioral sciences.* Belmont, CA: Brooks/Cole Publishing Company.

Paul, G.L. & Lentz, R.J. (1977). *Psychosocial treatment of chronic mental patients: Milieu vs. social learning programs.* Cambridge, MA: Harvard University Press.

Paul, G.L., Tobia, L.L., & Holly, B.L. (1972). Maintenance psychotropic drugs in the presence of active treatment programs: A triple-blind withdrawal study with long-term mental patients. *Archives of general psychiatry, 27,* 106-115.

Pepper, B. & Ryglewicz, H. (1984). *Advances in treating the young adolescent chronic patient.* San Francisco: Jossey-Bass.

Schaeffer, H.H. & Martin, L. (1966). Behavioral therapy for apathy of hospitalized schizophrenics. *Psychological Reports, 19,* 1147-1158.

Strossen, R.J., Coates, T.J., & Thoresen, C. (1979). Extending generalizability theory to single-subject designs. *Behavior Therapy, 10,* 606-614.

Tessler, R.C. & Goldman, H.H. (1982). *The chronically mentally ill: Assessing community support programs.* Cambridge, MA: Ballinger Publishing Company.

Thomas, E.J. (1984). *Designing interventions for the helping professions.* Beverly Hills, CA: Sage Publications.

Toward a National Plan for the Chronically Mentally Ill. (1980). Washington, D.C.: U.S. Department of Health and Human Services, Steering Committee on the Chronically Mentally Ill, publication no. (ADM) 81-1077.

Chapter 7
Research Designs for Studying the Chronically Mentally Ill: Studying the Person in the Environment

Claudia J. Coulton

Research designs on the chronically mentally ill can focus at several levels. Numerous studies have focused on the prevalence and distribution of psychiatric disorders, dysfunctional behavior, and service utilization, primarily using cross-sectional survey designs. Recently, we have also recognized that longitudinal survey designs are necessary to study chronicity, service utilization patterns, readmission rates, and behavioral change. These studies are epidemiological in their approach and provide both descriptive information and an opportunity for correlational analyses. Findings are useful for understanding the size and scope of a problem as well as initial information regarding the interrelationships among sociodemographic characteristics, psychiatric symptomatology, and service utilization and outcomes.

At the opposite end of the spectrum are clinical studies of the chronically mentally ill. Such studies, which tend to include only the patient or client who seeks treatment, focus on specific symptom patterns, behavioral disorders, subpopulation groups, or treatment settings. In-depth data collection may focus on the detailed aspects of behavior, personality, perception, and cognition, and the studies make possible a precise understanding of the characteristics of the clients receiving particular types of treatments. Such studies often focus also on the impact of specific treatment interventions on a specific group of clients. The designs for clinical studies tend to be experimental, quasi-experimental, or observational; occasionally, case study methodologies are also used. Ethnographic or other qualitative methods may also be useful.

This paper will focus on research questions regarding person-environment interaction. It will examine studies that fall between large epidemiological surveys and smaller clinical studies—studies that are interested in the relationship of chronically mentally ill individuals to their environments. Studies of the person in the environment are particularly important because they have the potential to contribute to our understanding of the chronically mentally ill beyond what can be learned through studying either the individual or environment separately. However, they are problematic due to methodological issues that arise in attempting to span these two levels of analysis.

THE PERSON-ENVIRONMENT FIT

The fit, or congruence, between psychiatric patients and their environments is crucial for several reasons. First, a disability or limitation in functioning is only a handicap (i.e., an interference) when the environment requires behaviors that an individual cannot perform. By definition, a handicap cannot exist when there is congruence between the individual and the environment. Further, several studies have shown how psychiatric patients have particular difficulty in adapting to new or changing environments (Alker, 1976; Moos, 1968; Gillis, 1977). Features of the environment that are easily managed by nonpsychiatric populations may be insurmountable for the individual who is chronically mentally ill.

Research on the person-environment relationship in the chronically mentally ill population is useful for several reasons. First, it would be useful to mental health personnel to measure people and environments along commensurate dimensions and then judge the extent to which these dimensions are important to their functioning. Such information would be particularly useful in discharge planning, or planning for placement of people in the community. Second, an understanding of the important aspects of person-environment congruence would be useful to consultants who work with environments that care for psychiatric patients or to those who help patients choose appropriate environments. Third, this kind of research could contribute to theoretical understanding of the relative importance of personal characteristics and environmental characteristics in understanding human well-being, social functioning, and the occurrence of behavior.

Within the last several years, Tom Holland, Virginia Fitch, and I completed a study of person-environment congruence between former mental patients and their community-care homes (Coulton et al., 1984a; Coulton et al., 1984b; Coulton et al., 1985). This study was supported by the Ohio Department of Mental Health. We measured psychiatric patients being discharged from state hospitals into community-care homes on 11 dimensions of their personal characteristics. We also measured their community-care environments along the same 11 dimensions. The 11 dimensions were derived primarily from those developed by Rudolf Moos in his study of community oriented programs (Moos, 1972). See table 1.

We found that the fit between the person and the environment of the community-care home, measured on selected dimensions, was a predictor of the patient's ability to function in the community as well as the likelihood of readmission to the hospital. Interestingly, we found that some discrepancies predicted readmission to the hospital while others were predictive of the person's community functioning. Readmission to the hospital was closely related to those aspects of misfit that would be of concern to the home operators; a patient's functioning was closely related to aspects of misfit that would provoke distress in the patient but not be seen as particularly disruptive for the home itself.

Readmission

For example, readmission was more likely when the patient differed from the environment in the negative direction on the dimensions of autonomy and personal problem orientation, in

Table 1

Dimensions of Person-Environment Congruence

Dimension	Content
Personal Problem Orientation	A person's need to discuss personal problems and the opportunities the environment provides to do so.
Anger and Aggression	A person's need to express anger and the extent to which the environment permits anger to be expressed.
Order and Organization	A person's need for neatness and organization and the presence of neatness and organization in the environment.
Control	The extent that rules of conduct and discipline are imposed on the person as compared with his desire to do this for himself.
Privacy	A person's desire for privacy and the privacy available in the environment.
Spontaneity	A person's desire to express feelings openly and the extent to which the environment encourages the open expression of feelings.
Autonomy	A person's need for independence and the extent to which independence is encouraged in the environment.
Involvement	The extent to which a person wants to be actively involved in day-to-day activities with others as compared with the extent this is encouraged in the environment.
Support	The extent to which support is available in an environment as compared with a person's desire for support.
Practical Orientation	A person's desire to learn practical skills and the extent to which the environment provides opportunities for learning practical skills.

the positive direction on spontaneity, and in either direction on order. In other words, patients whose capacities to act autonomously are minimal may be made quite anxious in environments that allow more autonomy than they can accept. Patients who are less willing to discuss personal problems than is expected by their environments may be viewed as uncooperative. A patient who is quite spontaneous and openly expresses feelings may be upsetting in a home where this is not the norm. Environments that provide either more or less order than the patient needs may result in a perception of either rebelliousness or confusion.

Level of Functioning

Unlike readmission, a patient's level of functioning was related to the patient-environment discrepancies in several areas.

Order. Patients who perceived a different amount of order in their environments than they preferred displayed less stability in community functioning.

Anger. Discrepancies between the person and environment on the dimension of anger also had a negative effect on functioning. Discrepancies in either direction were detrimental.

Autonomy. A patient's perception of fit on the autonomy dimension was also important. Particularly detrimental effects were associated with environments that demand more autonomy than the patient could tolerate.

Privacy. A lack of privacy as observed by the patient had a negative effect.

Practical Orientation. Patients' perceptions that there was too much practical orientation or emphasis on learning tasks and skills were associated with less stability of community functioning. This seemed to reflect the effects of excessive demands for performance on this sample.

Personal Orientation. Environments viewed by patients as giving too little attention to personal problems had a negative effect on functioning.

Control. When patients perceived too much or too little control in the environment, they displayed less stability in functioning.

In addition to the primary results of the studies, we were able to identify clusters of environmental characteristics that are common in different types of community-care homes (Coulton et al., 1985). Homes can be divided into four groups based on characteristics of their social environments. One type of home tended to be relatively unstructured and placed few demands on patients' autonomy and performance. At the other extremes were homes that could be characterized as total treatment environments that provided high levels of support, demanded large amounts of autonomy and learning, and had very structured programming. Other homes ranged somewhere in between these two extremes. Community-care homes cannot be considered a homogenous commodity in the environments they provide, and placement decisions should be made with careful knowledge of the environment and the selection of patients whose characteristics would be suitable for the particular homes.

PROBLEMS OF METHODOLOGY

Our studies of person-environment congruence raised a series of methodological problems that must be resolved if this type of research is to develop further.

One problem is how we can measure environments. Specifically, should we use the environment that manifests itself to the particular individual we are studying—in other words, the individual's subjective environment? Should we, instead, attempt to characterize the overall environment as perceived by all members of the situation? Or is it best to rely on objective observers who are not part of the environment? In a psychiatric environment, should we use the perceptions of both residents and staff to characterize the environment? In our study, we found wide differences in the degree to which a person's environmental congruence predicted outcome, depending on whether we used a patient's perception of the environment as the environmental measure or the perception of staff or objective observers. We found, for example, that a patient's perception of the environment was strongly predictive of the patient's functioning, whereas the staff's perception of the environment and how it fit with the patient was most predictive of whether the patient was returned to the hospital. Other studies have found that using averages of observers' perspectives or averages of patients' perspectives of the environmental measure yield different results than using each individual's own perception as the measure. Using psychiatric patients as informants about the environment poses additional problems due to their often impaired perception.

A second methodological issue is the method of quantifying person-environment congruence or discrepancy and how to use this measure statistically. Several methods have been tried, but each has limitations.

1. *A difference score.* Simple subtraction yields a score that reflects the discrepancy between the person and environment. This score will be reliable only if both the person and environment are measured without error or if there is no correlation between the two measures. Otherwise, the difference score will be less reliable than the component scores (Cronbach & Furbey, 1970).

2. *A residual score.* This reflects the portion of the variance in the person's score that cannot be predicted by the environment score, or vice versa (Kahana et al., 1980). A problem with this approach is that actual differences may exist between the person and environment but will not be reflected in the value of the residual if the rank ordering of persons on the two scales is the same.

3. *An interaction term.* The impact of the congruence would be accessed through the statistical interaction effect that is over and above the main effects of the person or environment alone (Kulka, 1979). This method avoids the problem of the unreliability of difference scores and the difficulties of residuals. However, it has the disadvantage of reducing degrees of freedom, since each concept requires three variables: the person's score, the environment, and

an interaction term. Further, if the person's score is correlated with the environment score, multicolinearity will be a problem.

A third issue in person-environment fit research has to do with the direction of the lack of congruence. There are problems both in portraying this direction statistically as well as conceptualizing the meaning of the direction of the discrepancy. This concept of directionability has been characterized as over-supply, under-supply or equal supply (French et al., 1974). It stands to reason that on some dimensions of person-environment congruence it would be equally harmful to have an environment that provides more than is needed (over-supply) or less than is needed (under-supply). On other dimensions, only an over-supply or an under-supply may be predictive of a negative outcome. In other instances, an over-supply may produce different results than an under-supply. For example, consider the dimension of autonomy: too much autonomy for the person in our study was found to have negative consequences for functioning. Additional research is needed to understand the intervening variables between excess autonomy and functioning. It is possible that excessive amounts of autonomy may lead to anxiety that produces increased symptomatology. Too little autonomy in our particular study was not shown to be a problem; however, this may be due to the fact that we were dealing with a severely disabled population. If the sample were drawn from a less disabled population and one of the outcome measures was learning or growth, the results would probably show that too little autonomy is a negative factor in growth or learning.

The representation of under-supply and over-supply in a statistical model is particularly problematic. In theory, under-supply and over-supply could be represented by including a curvilinear term in the model—for example, a polynominal might be used to represent both linear and curvilinear effects, and a squared or cubed term could be entered to represent a U- or S-shaped curve. However, while this may be ultimately feasible when measurement techniques improve, fitting a smooth curve with rough measurement is fairly difficult. We resolved this problem by including in our models a dummy variable (1,0) to represent either over-supply or under-supply. If the dummy variable made a significant contribution to the outcome, the direction of the discrepancy on the particular dimension was important in addition to the actual magnitude of the discrepancy. For some dimensions the dummy variable was not important, and we concluded that a discrepancy in either direction had an impact. When the dummy variable was important, it was often more important than the actual magnitude of the discrepancy. In these instances, based on the sign of the coefficient for the dummy variable, we concluded that either an over-supply or under-supply of the dimension was important in understanding the outcome.

It is conceivable, as well, that under-supplies and over-supplies may not always be two ends of a bipolar continuum. For example, research on staff-resident interaction in nursing homes has focused on the extent to which person-environment congruence in the area of independence is important (Kahana & Kiyak, 1984). Factor analysis has shown that the concept of independence may produce two dimensions (Kahana & Kiyak, 1980). It is possible that these dimensions represent a separate independence dimension and a dependence dimension. What this suggests, then, for a concept such as independence, is that people may be characterized orthogonally as preferring, needing, wanting, or desiring independence and as preferring, needing, wanting, or desiring dependence. It is conceivable that some people may want both high levels of independence and dependence, and that these desires may be met in different realms of their activities. Perhaps environments could also be characterized as providing high levels of opportunity for independence as well as providing high levels of opportunity for dependence. This would be an example of a situation in which what may previously have been understood as under-supply or over-supply of independence should now be represented as two separate dimensions that have a more precise relationship with some outcome. Detailed studies of all dimensions of environments that have been shown to be important may be needed to sort out the situations where bipolar continuums of under-supply and over-supply are not the proper conceptualization for the variable.

Studies of person-environment congruence encounter numerous practical problems, not the least of which is having sufficient variance in the environment. To achieve sufficient variance, it is typically necessary to study multiple environments, which makes objective measure of the environments by observers problematic. Often there are too few observers for each environment to have confidence that the measure is truly objective. It is also difficult to get an independent assessment of the preferences or characteristics of the person and still maintain a methodological distinction between personal preferences and personal perceptions of the environment. We do not understand how cognitive dissonance affects the person's perception of the environment and makes the environment seem more congruent than it actually is with himself or herself. Changing one's perception of an environment may be a method of coping. In studies of environments that people have been in for some time, the respondents may appear more congruent with the environment partly due to methods of coping such as denial or changing their perceptions. These methods of coping may have their own negative consequences, but it would obscure a relationship between person-environment congruence and a particular outcome. Thus the timing of the various measures of person-environment congruence and various outcomes is particularly important and apt to affect the conclusion drawn from the study.

CONCLUSION

For social workers and others who view their mission as the interface between people and their environments, it is vital to address the methodological problems of measurement, longitudinal design, and statistical modeling that are inherent in studies of person-environment congruence. This is particularly important in the study of the chronically mentally ill, who require special environments, modified environments, or prosthetic environments (Lawton, 1974). Such studies are likely to produce benefits in program planning, clinical work, and public policy.

REFERENCES

Alker, H. (1976). Is personality situation specific or intrapsychically consistent? In N. Endler and D. Magnusson (Eds.), *International psychology and personality*. New York: John Wiley and Sons, 564-576.

Coulton, C., Fitch, V., & Holland, T. (1985). A typology of social environments in community care homes. *Hospital and Community Psychiatry, 36,* 373-377.

Coulton, C., Holland T., & Fitch, V. (1984a). Person-environment congruence as a predictor of early rehospitalization from community care homes. *Psychosocial Rehabilitation Journal, 8,* 24-37.

Coulton, C., Holland, T., & Fitch, V. (1984b). Person-environment congruence and psychiatric patient outcome in community care homes. *Administration in Mental Health, 12,* 71-88.

Cronbach, L. & Furby, L. (1970). How we should measure change—or should we? *Psychological Bulletin, 74,* 68-80.

French, J., Rogers, W., & Cobb, S. (1974). Adjustment as person-environment fit. In G. Coelho, D. Hamburg, and J. Adams (Eds.), *Coping and adaptation*. New York: Basic Books.

Gillis, J. (1977). The effects of selected antipsychotic drugs on human judgment. *Current Therapeutic Research, 21,* 224-232.

Kahana, E., Hiang, J., & Felton, B. (1980). Alternative models of person-environment fit: Prediction of morale in three homes for the aged. *Journal of Gerontology, 35,* 584-595.

Kahana, E. & Kiyak, A. (1984). Attitudes and behavior of staff in facilities for aged. *Research in Aging, 6,* 395-416.

Kahana, E. & Kiyak, A. (1980). Antecedents, content and outcome of attitudes toward the elderly. Paper presented at 33rd Annual Scientific Meeting of the Gerontology Society, San Diego.

Kulka, R. (1979). Interaction as person-environment fit. *New Directions for Methodology of Behavioral Science, 2,* 55-71.

Lawton, M. (1974). Social ecology and the health of older people. *American Journal of Public Health, 64,* 257-260.

Moos, R. (1972). The community-oriented programs environment scale. *Community Mental Health Journal, 8,* 28-37.

Chapter 8
A Prospective Longitudinal Design to Study Provision of Community Service to Persons with Chronic Mental Illness

Phyllis Solomon

One of the original assumptions of the community mental health movement was that psychiatric patients discharged from state hospitals or those prevented from unnecessary hospitalization would receive mental health services in the community. As deinstitutionalization progressed, however, concerns arose as to whether the chronic mental patient was being served by community agencies. A myriad of unanswered questions were raised concerning service provision to persons with chronic mental illness. This paper describes a longitudinal design intended to answer those questions.

The design that is proposed is termed a *prospective longitudinal design*. To illustrate the efficacy of this type of design, two studies will be used as examples—one a study of discharged psychiatric patients; the other a study, currently in progress, of patients seen in a psychiatric emergency room but not referred for inpatient care.

RESEARCH QUESTIONS

The following major questions are posed for researchers in community mental health services:

1. Who are the discharged patients? Who are the patients using a psychiatric emergency room but not referred for in-

patient care?

2. Are the patients referred to community-based mental health services?
3. Who receives aftercare services? Who receives post-psychiatric emergency room services?
4. What kinds of services do they receive?
5. Do these aftercare services meet the needs of discharged patients? Do these community-based services meet the needs of those previously seen in a psychiatric emergency room who are diverted from hospitalization?
6. What is happening in the lives of these patients in the community?
7. Do the services the patients receive affect their community tenure, rehospitalization, hospitalization or return to the psychiatric emergency room?

RESEARCH DESIGN

The *prospective* nature of the design is dictated by the need to obtain informed consent from the patients in order to protect their right to confidentiality. Obtaining informed consent increases the time and cost of conducting the research, but, at the same time, it enriches the data that are obtained. Informed consent can legitimately be sought from hospitalized patients. In Ohio, where the research was conducted, competency is a separate court action from involuntary commitment. Very few patients in state hospitals are involuntarily committed, and even fewer have been adjudicated to be incompetent. For those who had been adjudicated to be incompetent, which strictly speaking is a legal concept, we sought consent from their designated guardian.

The *longitudinal* nature of the design lies in the tracking of the cohort from an index date for a set time-frame from that date—that is, one year from the index date—to determine the nature, amount, and types of services received. In the study of aftercare services to discharged patients, the index date was defined as their date of hospital discharge for the hospitalization in which they entered the study (Solomon, Gordon, & Davis,

1984). In the study of patients who were seen in emergency rooms, the index date was the date of the emergency room evaluation for which they entered the study.

Because the focus of these studies is on the receipt of community services, the cohort was tracked through an entire community mental health service delivery system and its major auxiliary services—county welfare, Social Security Administration, Bureau of Vocational Rehabilitation, and Visiting Nurses Association—to record the dates, types, and amounts of service received. In the psychiatric emergency room study, alcohol and drug abuse agencies were also included because there is a high incidence of these problems among persons with chronic mental illness. An entire mental health service delivery system was included in the study by setting geographical parameters that correspond to the legislated area for the local community mental health system.

Target Populations

The target populations in both studies are subpopulations of persons with chronic mental illness who are potentially eligible for the community service system under study. One study was of discharged state psychiatric patients; the other study, currently being conducted, is of those individuals who came to a psychiatric emergency room (that was publicly funded to serve the entire county) but were not referred for inpatient care.

(The current study was originally designed to examine individuals who sought state psychiatric admissions but were deemed not to need hospitalization. However, major policy and program changes in the system necessitated redesigning the study. All noncourt referrals were required to be prescreened at the county-wide psychiatric emergency room, and only those assessed to need hospitalization were to be sent to the state hospital. Although the location and the nature of the setting changed, both studies were conceived to examine subgroups of persons with chronic mental illness who were noninstitutionalized or, more specifically, being diverted from institutionalization.)

STUDY 1. DISCHARGED PSYCHIATRIC PATIENTS: THE AFTERCARE STUDY

Sampling Procedures

For the study of discharged psychiatric patients, six months were required to obtain the cohort of 550 patients to be tracked. All inpatients at two state psychiatric receiving hospitals at the start of sampling as well as those subsequently admitted who met the study criteria were eligible for participation in the study. Study criteria prescribed that patients be:

1. aged 18 to 65 years;
2. a resident of Cuyahoga County;
3. not discharged to long-term psychiatric or nursing-home care, thus eligible to use the aftercare system under study;
4. in the hospital longer than 24 hours.

Only 20 percent of the patients approached refused to participate. It was felt that there was no systematic bias in the order in which patients entered the hospital. This was statistically confirmed in that the sample did not significantly differ from the total hospital populations for the time period on the following variables: type of admissions, previous hospitalization, gender, and age.

Nature of Data Collected

Data were collected to reflect the full experience of individuals involved in the public mental health aftercare system from hospitalization to community living to possible rehospitalization. Sources of study data included hospital records, social workers providing inpatient care who completed specific study forms, the computerized management information system of the county mental health board, community agency records, and former patients themselves.

Inpatient Experience. From hospital medical records, information was gathered on clinical and social demographic characteristics and on inpatient services received. Three forms were completed by the inpatient social worker as near to the patient's date of discharge as possible.

- A *functional assessment instrument* to measure expected social functioning after discharge.
- A *service needs assessment,* which was based on the components of the NIMH Community Support System. The range of services was developed into specific service programs. The social workers used this form to assess the post-discharge service needs of all study participants. Service needs were operationally defined as: (1) necessary for the patient to be self sufficient or to be working towards self sufficiency, and (2) appropriate to the patient's level of functioning at the time of discharge. The social worker was to identify those services meeting the criteria of needed services, regardless of whether the patient had received them prior to hospitalization or not and regardless of whether they actually existed or not.
- A *referral linkage form* on which the social worker indicated the procedures they performed during hospitalization to link that patient with aftercare services. These activities included inpatient social workers having telephone contact, face-to-face contact with an agency worker, arranging transportation and scheduling an appointment with an agency.

Community Experience. To determine the date, amount, and type of services that each cohort member received, each participating agency received the entire list of names and aliases of all participating clients.

The method of obtaining data on the clients that the agencies had served varied by agency. The largest agencies were on the computerized management information system of the county mental health board. Each agency provided the research team with the identifying numbers of the clients it had served. These numbers were used to extract the necessary information from the data base.

Some of the agencies not on the computerized information system completed data forms developed for the study; other agencies allowed the research staff to review their case records and extract the relevant information. In some instances, the agencies' records contained service tickets indicating the amount, date, and type of service delivered, making data extraction more efficient. The agencies from whom the specific amount of service was not available in the record were still able to estimate the amount of time for each type of service provided.

The Cuyahoga County Welfare Department and the Social Security Administration provided data from their computerized systems. The nature of their data was different from that of other agencies. County Welfare provided information on authorized service within our designated study period. Social Security provided income program and payment information for the study period.

The County Mental Health Board employs service definitions that all mental health contract agencies use for their service coding schemes. The research team used these definitions to develop a coding scheme for the service data that were collected. However, variations in the ways in which agencies defined and coded their services influenced the list of service types that was used for the study.

Readmissions. Dates of all rehospitalizations for the year of tracking were obtained from the state hospital records for all cohort members in the study. Although there was a lack of clarity as to what conceptually constitutes rehospitalization (Solomon & Doll, 1979) and its corollary community tenure, we employed these as outcome indicators in the study, for the goals of the community mental health aftercare system are to increase community tenure and reduce rehospitalization.

Patient In-depth Interview. To supplement the data collected from the hospitals and community agencies, in-depth interviews were conducted with a random subsample of the 550 study participants. Through the more qualitative data of the interview, we were able to take a closer look at the problems of being a former patient. The interview also provided us with information on how and when they used other community resources.

Interview schedules were reviewed by COPE (Client-Oriented Program Evaluation), a consumer group from Hill House (a psychosocial rehabilitation agency in Cleveland) that does evaluation, and by a self-help program organized by former psychiatric patients. Their suggestions were utilized in the final interview schedule.

The computer selected a random sample of 100 members from the original cohort to be interviewed. The interviews were conducted approximately one year after discharge from the hospital. Those interviewed were paid ten dollars. Fifty-nine interviews were completed. Some cohort members were found but refused to be interviewed, some failed to show for appointments, and others lived too far away to be interviewed.

Letters were initially sent to the addresses to which patients had been discharged. If that first letter failed to get a response, another was sent to the address of the significant other given at admission. If we had phone numbers, we called either the patient or the significant other, or both. For patients who received service, we were able to obtain more recent addresses from agencies. In all inquiries, we never revealed the purpose of the study to anyone other than the client.

STUDY 2. PSYCHIATRIC EMERGENCY ROOM STUDY

The purpose of this study was to determine the nature and amounts of service received by individuals who came to a psychiatric emergency room of a general hospital and were not referred for inpatient care. This service was contracted by the local public mental health funding authority to conduct prescreening for state psychiatric hospitalization.

Sampling Procedure

Two-and-a-half months were required to obtain a cohort of 114. Research staff were stationed at the unit in order to obtain consents, but coverage was contingent on peak times and availability of staff. Eligibility criteria similar to those of the previous study were employed so the samples would be comparable. To be eligible for the current study, cohort members could not be referred for inpatient care, either psychiatric or detoxification. This study had a 30 percent refusal rate. A $5 incentive was given to participate in the study.

Nature of Data Collected

The procedures employed in this study were similar to those in the aftercare study. Data were extracted from psychiatric emergency room records. However, since that information was minimal, a short interview was conducted with the patient at the time the consent was obtained. The interview data consisted of clinical and social demographic characteristics and prior services received, both inpatient and outpatient. Research staff also collected data concerning the referral process from the psychiatric emergency room to the community agency. Also, history on prior psychiatric hospitalizations was obtained from the Ohio Department of Mental Health's computerized information system. A psychiatric assessment using the Global Assessment Scale, by Spitzer, Gibbon and Endicott, was to be completed by the staff psychiatrists, but few forms were completed. We did not deem extensive assessments such as service needs and social functioning to be appropriate, given the minimal contact with the client by the psychiatric emergency room staff.

The nature of the community service data was the same as for the aftercare study; however, the tracking period was three months for the receipt of services and six months for hospitalizations and psychiatric emergency room returns. Agencies on the computerized information system provided researchers with printouts of the services delivered to the clients they served. All returns to the psychiatric emergency room for six months after the patient's index date were obtained by reviewing the records of the psychiatric emergency room. Also, the dates of public psychiatric hospitalizations for the six-month interval from the index date were obtained.

Approximately six months after their entrance into the study, we attempted to contact the entire cohort for an extensive interview. We were able to complete interviews with two-thirds of the cohort members. Contact procedures similar to those in the aftercare study were employed. We contacted meal sites in an attempt to find some of the 8 percent of the cohort members who were homeless. Only one homeless person was found and interviewed.

MAJOR ADVANTAGES AND DISADVANTAGES OF THIS DESIGN AS COMPARED TO ALTERNATIVE DESIGNS

There are a number of advantages that this design has over other types. The longitudinal aspect of the design permitted us to obtain actual dates, nature, and amounts of services over a period of time. A cross-sectional survey design would have relied on the recall of clients for these data. Obtaining these service data from agency records increased the validity of the data due to the fact that agencies require these data for reporting and billing. Using actual amounts of services resulted in interval level data that enabled us to employ more powerful statistics than we could have with client-reported service utilization.

Obtaining the dates of services received and readmissions for the one-year follow-up period enabled us to analyze the relationship and sequence of these factors. For example, dates and amounts of services received and dates of rehospitalizations enabled us to determine the impact of the intensity of services received on community tenure and how aftercare service utilization influenced whether a patient was readmitted.

The longitudinal nature of the design furthermore made it possible for us to compare our results to a similar aftercare study conducted earlier in Kentucky (Kirk, 1977). Kirk's study was a longitudinal retrospective, rather than prospective, study. The advantages discussed to this point apply to the longitudinal rather than the prospective nature of the study. However, a retrospective study would not have obtained signed consent forms from the study participants. The Office of Program Evaluation and Research of the Ohio Department of Mental Health would not have approved these studies for funding without this protection of human subjects, even though they were aware that obtaining consents greatly increased the costs of the two studies.

For the aftercare study, two full-time research assistants worked for six months in the two participating hospitals to gain consent from sample members. The psychiatric emergency room study took a number of interviewers two-and-a-half months, working different shifts, to gain the consents of this cohort. The task of gaining consent not only added to the cost but also to the duration of both studies. To obtain the service data, we had to wait for a year past the last date of the discharge of the aftercare cohort and six months from the last date of the emergency visit for the psychiatric emergency room cohort.

Several agencies reviewed the proposal for protection of subjects and carefully scrutinized our detailed consent form. The Social Security Administration requested us to specify on the consent form the particular data elements we would be requesting from them. We had to provide copies of our consent forms to such agencies as the Social Security Administration, County Welfare and a public general hospital prior to their releasing data to us. The general hospital, as well as the state hospitals and other agencies, placed the consent forms in the clients' agency records.

Just prior to the start of the aftercare study, the Ohio Department of Mental Health issued administrative rules on the release of client information for community mental health agencies, stipulating that consent forms were valid for only ninety days. Since it would have been inordinately expensive and impractical to obtain new consent forms every ninety days, we met with the legal department of the Ohio Department of Mental Health. The opinion of the legal department was that the 90-day requirement was not applicable to our project. With this ruling, agencies agreed to participate.

Without the consent forms, some agencies would not have agreed to participate. Fearing that they would be compared with other agencies in amounts of services delivered, agencies were afraid to participate in the study. Confidentiality of client data was used as a major focus of concern by these agencies, but with consent forms this issue was diminished. We helped to alleviate agencies' fears by assuring them that we were interested in the total service delivery system and not in evaluating specific agencies. Eventually, every agency that was asked to participate in both studies did so.

The need to obtain consent forms potentially biased the sample toward those who were willing to participate. But, as previously noted, in the aftercare study such a bias was determined not to be a problem.

The prospective nature of the aftercare study did have certain advantages over a retrospective design. Hospital social workers were able to assess the functioning and service needs of the aftercare cohort members, as well as document the actual procedures employed to link the patients with agencies at discharge. These data retrospectively would have been highly unreliable and invalid and, in most cases, not retrievable. These data greatly expanded the questions that could be addressed in the study. For example, the study related a client's level of functioning and need for service to the amounts and nature of services received. Also, the study evaluated the extent to which clients received the type of services they were assessed as needing at discharge. These data also enabled us to look at the types of referral linkage procedures that enhanced post-discharge contact with agencies. Similarly, the psychiatric emergency room study will assess referral procedures.

In the psychiatric emergency room study, being on the spot at the time of the psychiatric assessment enabled us to collect data that the emergency room does not typically record—for example, who accompanied the client to the emergency room. Also, we were able to administer an interview with the client at this time, giving us additional information such as prior service use and clients' perceptions of how they came to the hospital. We attempted to administer a rather long interview but found that many clients would not complete it. So as not to bias the sample, we made only part of the interview required for the incentive payment fee and left the remainder of the interview optional.

The follow-up interviews that were conducted in both studies consisted of a survey design study within the larger studies. These interviews were conducted approximately six months after the psychiatric emergency room visit and a year after hospital discharge. The interviews helped to explain and enhance the more quantitative service data by providing a consumer perspective on the amounts and nature of services received. For example, consumers informed us that they were satisfied with the nature and amounts of services offered. They desired to be self-reliant and not dependent on services. The low levels of services received by clients were as much contingent on how agencies provided services as how clients choose to use the aftercare system of services. The interviews also provided information on those who elected not to use the publicly funded aftercare system. However, the nature of information that can be obtained on the private delivery system is very limited in comparison to the public, for the service data on private systems is dependent on the client's report. It is not feasible to obtain actual dates, nature, and amounts of services from the private sector.

AFTERCARE STUDY RESULTS

It is important to present the results of the aftercare study in a general way. We found that a relatively high proportion of cohort members did make contact with community mental health agencies after discharge. Those who received services received maintenance services such as chemotherapy, case management, and counseling services. Few received the more rehabilitative services such as day treatment, residential services, psychosocial rehabilitation, or vocational rehabilitation. Also, they received very low levels of services—a median of 12 hours in the year following discharge and prior to rehospitalization. Given the amounts of services received, it is not surprising that the receipt of aftercare services did increase community tenure but did not prevent hospitalization. The nature and amounts of service that these patients received served to support or maintain them in the community but did little to rehabilitate or change their life style of intermittent rehospitalization. Thirty-eight percent of the cohort were rehospitalized in one year. There was no significant difference in the rates of return for those who received services and those who did not: 36 percent for clients receiving services, 42 percent for those not. However, those who received services had longer community tenure. Several publications provide detailed results of the study (Solomon & Davis, 1985; Solomon, Gordon & Davis, 1983; 1984a; 1984b; 1984c; 1984d).

CONCLUSION

A longitudinal prospective design has certain advantages and disadvantages over a retrospective one. Given the requirements of protection of human subjects, we did not have the latitude to select. Employing the same design with two subgroups of persons with chronic mental illness will enable us to compare these two subgroups in terms of utilization of services and their perspectives on services as well as their lives in general.

Both studies discussed in this paper were funded by the Office of Program Evaluation and Research, Ohio Department of Mental Health.

REFERENCES

Kirk, S. (1977). Who gets aftercare? A study of patients discharged from state hospitals in Kentucky. *Hospital and Community Psychiatry, 28*(2), 109-114.

Solomon, P. & Davis, J. (1985). Meeting community service needs of discharged psychiatric patients. *Psychiatric Quarterly, 57*(1), 11-17.

Solomon, P. & Doll, W. (1979). The varieties of readmission: The case against the use of recidivism rates as a measure program effectiveness. *American Journal of Orthopsychiatry, 49*(2), 218-239.

Solomon, P., Gordon, B., & Davis, J. (1983). An assessment of aftercare services within a community mental health system. *Psychosocial Rehabilitation Journal, 7*(2), 33-39.

Solomon, P., Gordon, B., & Davis, J. (1984a). *Community services to discharged psychiatric patients.* Springfield, IL: Charles C. Thomas.

Solomon, P., Gordon, B., & Davis, J. (1984b). Discharged state hospital patients' characteristics and use of care: Effect on community tenure. *American Journal of Psychiatry, 141*(12), 1566-1570.

Solomon P., Gordon, B., & Davis, J. (1984c). Assessing service needs of the discharged patient. *Social Work in Health Care, 10,* 61-69.

Solomon P., Gordon, B., & Davis, J. (1984d). Differentiating psychiatric readmissions. *American Journal of Orthopsychiatry, 54*(3), 426-435.

Chapter 9
Research Strategy, Network, and Process in a Twelve-Year Longitudinal Study

Steven P. Segal and David Cohen

The problems of implementing the search process in a longitudinal study have received scant attention in the literature (Mednick & Baert, 1981; Schulsinger, Mednick, & Knop, 1981). This paper details the search process used in a twelve-year longitudinal study of 427 former mental patients residing in California sheltered-care facilities in 1973. Its focus is not on conceptual issues related to design but rather with those aspects that present the researcher with the most formidable obstacles. Although these obstacles can sometimes be surmounted by a researcher's experience and imagination, a systematic approach to implementation will help to accomplish the goals of the longitudinal study.

Ideally, an investigator designs a longitudinal study that will recapture a maximum number of sample members. This is done by incorporating inducements for sample members to continue their involvement, recording accurately all necessary identifying information (including birth date and social security number), as well as the name and address of a person who will usually know how to contact the sample member. The investigator also obtains signed consent forms authorizing organizations with confidential records to release locational information—for example, current addresses—to the researcher. (Each consent form should have an expiration date extending two years beyond the anticipated start of the follow-up study.)

154

Yet, even with inducements and releases, a study is likely to encounter many obstacles to locating sample members. In the absence of an ideal preplanned situation, search problems increase geometrically in inverse proportion to the quality of subject identifiers. Even in a well-planned study, the researcher will have to locate missing sample members. Although the proportion of missing or hard-to-locate sample members will vary depending on the characteristics of the sample surveyed, if the search process itself has no preplanning, the researcher is likely to waste precious time and resources.

"REINTEGRATING THE MENTALLY ILL": A FOLLOW-UP STUDY

"Reintegrating the Mentally Ill" (Segal & Aviram, 1978) was a well-designed sample population survey of all former mental patients in California who in 1973 were residing in sheltered-care facilities, but the survey was never meant to be a longitudinal investigation. Yet, ten years after the initial survey, we discovered that all consent forms signed by the study participants had been filed by sheltered care facility, not by alphabetical order. A simple clerical mistake thus opened the possibility of tracing each of the participants back to the facilities in which they had lived in 1973. Since only two or three individuals had been interviewed in each facility, this filing error made it possible in most cases to link a given name to an interview.

The projected study was intended to be a twelve-year follow-up of 427 mentally disabled adults who lived in sheltered-care homes throughout California during the summer of 1973. The study was to document the health, mental health, and social-services experiences of this cohort and determine how they have fared socially and psychologically. In addition, it would study the fates of their 217 sheltered-care facilities. The research, based on interviews with facility residents and managers who comprised the original sample, was intended to provide one of the first longitudinal views of sheltered-care residents (a high-risk group from the perspective of deinstitutionalization policy), facilities, and the neighborhoods that host them.

As of this writing, 85 percent of the living sample of residents and 75 percent of the managers have been interviewed. We have accounted for the whereabouts of over 91 percent of the original sample of residents and 83 percent of the original manager sample.

The Segal and Avram survey is an example of a longitudinal study that was not preplanned; as such, it illustrates the most difficult situation that can be encountered. Our experiences should help all longitudinal researchers to minimize the impact of Murphy's Law and to plan more successful studies.

Human Subjects Reviews

In such a longitudinal study, especially one that looks at several organizations, requirements concerning the protection of participants and confidentiality of information are quite stringent. Researchers should be prepared for the most thorough and critical investigations of their data-collection strategies. Problems involve access to locational information possessed by various health and social service organizations, ability to obtain informed consent from a disabled population, precautions to protect the privacy and dignity of participants, participant remuneration, and several other difficult questions. We were able to develop guidelines for the highest standards of protection of subjects through our participation in, and evaluation by, over 25 human-subject review boards. A separate document describes experiences with these lengthy and detailed reviews and some of the questions they raise about the conduct of social research (Segal & Kaplan, 1985).

Mental health researchers concerned with protecting the privacy of their sources and the confidentiality of the information they collect should consider applying for the confidentiality certificate authorized under Section 303(a) of the Public Health Service Act. The Act states:

the Secretary [of Health and Human Services] may authorize persons engaged in research on mental health...

to protect the privacy of individuals who are the subject of such research....Persons so authorized to protect the privacy of such individuals may not be compelled in any Federal, State, or local civil, criminal, administrative, legislative or other proceedings to identify such individuals.

STAGES OF THE STUDY

To complete this longitudinal study, three tasks were necessary: a follow-up strategy, an extensive search network, and an individual investigatory process. We describe each below.

Follow-up Strategy

We first needed to compile lists of the individuals who had been interviewed in 1973 and addresses of the sheltered-care facilities where the interviews had taken place. To compile those lists, we proceeded in several steps.

Confirming Subject Name. We interpreted the names of residents and facility managers or owners from their signatures on consent forms. When we were uncertain about a signature, we gave staff evaluation sheets and asked them to list, without consulting each other, what they thought the person's name was and how it should be spelled. The most frequently guessed name in this "name that subject" game was then considered to be the original sample member's name. We retain alternate guesses for future search purposes. Another tactic was to enlarge difficult signatures and have staff and facility informants view them. Microscopic evaluations were also done on these signatures, with consultation from a forensic graphologist.

An urban telephone book can be used to check the spelling of difficult names. Staff members of different backgrounds were also helpful in identifying ethnic names. A staff member's indignant statement—such as, "That's not Raparound it's Rappaport!"—was often the key to finding someone.

Confirming Subject Identity. If two or more subjects of the same sex were interviewed in a given facility, each name was attached to the possible alternate profile. Thus "Jane Seymour"' or "Jeannie Simmons," two possible interpretations of a signature, might have been interviewed in Facility 234, in which another woman was interviewed. One of these interviewees was black, 55 years old, and married, while the other was white, 45 years old, and single. Jane Seymour/Jeannie Simmons was one of these two, and we hoped to clarify her identity by interviewing the manager of the original facility. Our plan was to work from the original facility, using it as a source to confirm names and identities. Because we lacked birth dates and social security numbers, confirmation was quite difficult. We did, however, know our subjects' age and source of support in 1973.

Even with the correct spelling of a name, birth date, and social security number, confirming an identity of individuals in marginal populations may be difficult—especially if they do not wish to be found out. One of our sample members had 15 names, four social security numbers, and ten different dates of birth.

False leads can be costly and demoralizing to staff. We traced one individual for a year from northern California to Los Angeles, through moves to three different cities in the state of Washington, to a rural farm section of California, only to confirm that we had found the wrong person.

Searching From More Specific to More General Resources. After obtaining whatever information we could from the original facility, we gradually expanded our search to cover information provided by the mental health community and the broader health and social service networks. Finally, we approached the more general information listings available to the public, such as motor vehicles and voter registration. We chose this specific-to-general strategy because of the relatively disabled character of our resident sample. We assumed that keeping the search confined to the smallest geographic area and population would eliminate the problem of false leads, at least until we were sure that we had identified the proper person from the sample. In situations where we doubted if an individual was an index case, we made identities contingent upon a double confirmation with two independent sources verifying that the person had in fact lived at the facility at the time of the interview and matched the profile of the interviewee on significant or unique identifiers such as signature, employment of their father, or place of birth.

Locating the Original Facility. This we accomplished by cross-referencing our list with the current state licensing list of community-care facilities. We searched in *Haynes Reverse Telephone Directory* for the address of every facility not listed in the state's community-care licensing book or regular telephone directories. The reverse directory lists telephone numbers by address instead of customer names. This search was necessary for two reasons. First, no facilities were licensed by the state at the time of the original study, in the summer of 1973, and many facilities since then had chosen to remain unlicensed despite the state's efforts to upgrade residential care standards. Unlicensed facilities maintained a low profile and often had a telephone listed as a personal phone of the current owner or manager—usually a different individual and telephone number than in the original facility contact, an individual unknown to the study. Second, some facilities had moved, and information about their location would most likely come from the person currently occupying the residence. This contact sometimes confirmed the correct spelling of the original manager/owner's name, further enabling us to trace managers who had left the sheltered-care business.

Locating Owners/Managers. This task was usually done by contacting the facilities, but it was also aided by community-care home operators' associations, state licensing bureaus, mental health professionals, reviews of property tax records, and the thorough use of one's search network (see below).

Broadening the Search. We broadened our follow-up search strategy in two ways: (1) working from smaller to larger geographical areas, and (2) working from higher probability to lower probability contact sources. The goal is to obtain all possible true leads and avoid false leads.

The advantage in using the first strategy is that one is more likely to find people who know the sample member in the local area. One may thus reduce the probability of getting a false lead on another person with the same name and approximate age as the index case. Also, one is more likely to get better cooperation with a smaller number of people on a search list, since it is easier for an organization to search for one rather than twenty records.

Higher probability contact sources help to confirm identities. If one knows that the target sample will probably have more contacts with a given organization than another organization, it is more productive to start with the high contact source. For example, given our 1973 estimates, we expected approximately 25 percent of our resident sample to have yearly contact with a county mental health agency. We thus had a rather comprehensive way of beginning to trace our sample members in a different place than they were living 12 years before. Further, mental health records of an individual with the same name and age as one of our index cases often have a listing of current and previous addresses. If one of the latter was the facility where the index case was interviewed in 1973, we had a partial confirmation of the person's identity, as well as, sometimes, other information that could facilitate the search: telephone number, relative's name and address, or individual identifiers such as date of birth and social security number.

"Cold Calls." While much of the search occurs on the telephone, it is necessary to have a field interviewer who visits all address leads of people who cannot be reached by phone or have not responded to successive mail requests. The interviewer should be prepared to carry out an interview if he or she finds a person home and consent is obtained for the interview. The interviewer should be prepared to seek leads from neighbors without compromising the potential study participants, check for any confirmation that an individual is still living at an address, leave notes at the address requesting that the possible index case contact the principal investigator, and be ready to explain the aims of the study to all information sources (in our situation, due partly to concerns expressed by human subjects committees, this explanation had to omit any reference to mental illness). It is also crucial that the interviewer possess official identification, business card, and letter of introduction from the project director to facilitate any queries that a potential source may wish to make concerning the project or the interviewer's authenticity.

Establishing a Search Network

The second major component of the study involves "casting a broad net." To do this, one needs access to a network of information systems. The amount and ease of access to information systems depends largely on the official status of the study and the study organization; thus, state agencies conducting studies for official purposes have considerable ease of access.

Our 1973 study was originally funded by the California State Department of Health and Welfare and is currently conducted under the auspices of the California State Department of Social Services and Mental Health. The study is also sponsored by the National Institute of Mental Health and funded by the Robert Wood Johnson Foundation. Given this sponsorship, we were able to develop a search network in California that included access to the State Department of Mental Health's State Hospital Management Information System, the State Department of Criminal Justice's listings of individuals in state prisons and county jails, the state Department of Motor Vehicles, the state Department of Vital Statistics, state and county professional organizations, as well as licensing bodies, county voter registration listings, county departments of mental health and social services, and county offices of the public guardian. When we obtained a reasonable valid indication that an individual had moved out of state, we conducted national searches. For the latter, we relied on the Social Security Administration, the Veterans Administration, and the Federal Bureau of Investigation. We also relied on state departments of mental health, of motor vehicles, and of vital statistics in over 15 states. Without the cooperation of these agencies in our search network, the study would not have been possible.

Despite our success with these agencies and departments, we have discovered five reasons why one cannot rely solely on information systems in the search network:

- Search results may be unreliable

- Access to information systems may be limited or unavailable
- Information in a system may be out of date
- Systems vary in the types of information they are able to provide
- Systems vary in their robustness.

Some comments follow on each of these problems.

Unreliability of Search. If the same listing is searched more than once, some subjects missed the first time will be found. This occurs whether the list is computerized or noncomputerized, and does not necessarily depend on how well-meaning and how committed are the serving agencies or the personnel who carry out the search. For example, our first search of the State Department of Mental Health's computerized system yielded no leads, yet independent searches in each state hospital turned up five people residing in these hospitals. A second search of the same system yielded additional leads. There is no question that those who searched for us tried their best to do the job, but there may well be an inherent flaw in looking through large lists for a large number of names. Consequently, it is necessary to search the same list several times.

In our recent returns to state hospitals to abstract the records of individuals who had been hospitalized during the past 12 years, the medical records officers, remembering us, have often been quite astonished to find that the number of people whom we have found with records at their hospital has sometimes been as high as six times the number they were originally able to provide.

The search-list unreliability problem extends to all sources: vital statistics, motor vehicles, Medi-Cal, Social Security, and so on. It is crucial, therefore, to limit the number of people for whom an individual must search. We achieved this by focusing on smaller geographical units first and by splitting the lists for statewide units so as to reduce the burden on each agency by the positive leads obtained from other agencies when we exchanged the split lists.

Limited or Unavailable Access. Negotiating access to information systems is one thing; gaining access to them is another.

It may take up to a year and a half, including several human subjects reviews, to obtain access to a registry. A key component of this access problem concerns the procedure, which is sanctioned under the Freedom of Information Act, of having an agency with an information system send letters to potential sample members on behalf of the investigator. The outcome of this procedure raises serious problems for the researcher, who may often not know whether a letter has been returned to the agency, whether an address is not accurate because the person has moved, whether the person refused to participate in the study, whether the person ever received the letter, or whether the person might wish to participate in the study but is unable to respond to a letter (not an infrequent occurrence among the chronically disabled). One cannot expect a woman in the midst of a major depression, who has been lying in a single-room occupancy hotel bed in her own feces and urine for three weeks (as was the case with one of our sample members), to respond to an agency's letter of request for an interview.

For many agencies, the letter procedure is the only option permitted by law. Other agencies choose this option in their human subjects review and become convinced of its lack of utility only when a low response rate occurs. In one case, an organization turned up 97 leads in their information system, but an extreme effort to make the letter procedure work could arrange only three interviews. That figure contrasts with an interview response rate over 90 percent when our own search teams made contacts independently in the same geographic area. In this situation, the human subjects committee reversed its opinion, a reversal which took more than a year to happen.

Human subjects objections are not the only problems of information-system access. Some data sets, such as the National Death Registry, require an application process and a minimum fee. Thus for a small study they may not be worth consulting. Further, some data sets may also require an exact date of birth, or at minimum the month and year of birth, to process a search. If a researcher possesses only a patient's age at original interview, 12 searches, one for each month, would be necessary.

Noncontemporary Information. Information obtained in the search is rarely up to date. It provides a starting point—such as a relative's name and address— and usually moves one forward in time in terms of the period one is searching to find a sample member. In effect, one obtains a place at which to find information that is more contemporary than the original starting point.

Different Types of Information. Information systems provide different types of leads. For example, a criminal justice system might not yield a specific address unless someone is in a state prison or other jail. It may, however, offer a geographic lead such as where the person was last seen, so that one may redirect the search geographically.

A system may offer a last address at which the person was served. Such addresses, especially with a disadvantaged, transient, and mobile population, rarely allow one to consult a telephone directory or telephone operator to make a direct contact with the potential sample member. On the other hand, such addresses provide a point of mail contact or allow for a reverse directory search to locate neighbors who might know the individual. Such addresses also permit unannounced visits ("cold calls") to people who do not respond to any mail contact and cannot be reached by telephone.

Another important use of system information is to locate people who are under the wing, so to speak, of a family member. It is not infrequent for a chronically mentally ill person to move in with a relative or a friend and disappear from all public listings. Their mail is sent to their friend's address, in care of their friend. In this situation, it is almost impossible to locate someone unless one has a lead indicating that the friend is a forwarding point. In many cases, therefore, one's search efforts must be broadened to include names of friends and relatives— persons whom one must find in order to find the sample member.

Robustness. General information systems vary greatly in their robustness. By *robustness* we refer to the type of information necessary to carry out a search and the amount of error the system will tolerate in this information and still yield substantial positive leads. For example, many systems can only search by date of birth and cannot use a name or age. Some systems allow a search by name, but only provide leads related to the specific name. Common names were often a problem. For example, one system will only pull the first 16 listings of persons with the same name and will not go further unless given a birth date.

The criminal justice system has a computer program called Soundex, which enables them to provide leads about names which sould like the name one is searching, but which must have an identical first letter. If one works from handwritten samples, such a tool is important—although not all-inclusive. An "alternative spell" program would be helpful but was not available on any search system we used. A robust system might enable one to search more than one spelling or a second variation of a given name, which is useful when subjects use more than one variation of their names. Several of our sample members used three or more names.

Robustness also refers to the time period covered by the information system. The National Death Registry, for example, covered only one-quarter of the time period we were interested in. In addition, many organizations delete names of clients from their records when they have not had contact with them for a given number of years. This procedure, spurred on by varying state and county legal mandates for confidentiality, often results in the destruction of records for people who are no longer active with one local agency but are active with other agencies performing similar functions in the same area.

In sum, the leads obtained from an information system must be viewed as clues in an investigatory process. One may get lucky with information leading to an immediate contact or, more likely, one obtains a lead which may be parlayed into an eventual contact. The strategy of a follow-up study is to use the search network to obtain whatever leads possible on each individual, to follow those leads, and approximately four to six months later, to resubmit to the same agencies to repeat the searches. This way, one controls for unreliability of the search and age of the information, and as search requests are sent to more than one system, the quality of the information submitted to other systems can be updated. As birth dates and social security numbers are obtained and correct name spellings confirmed, these can be cross-referenced with the information in the other systems one is using, thus building a comprehensive search network that becomes quite effective, if not efficient.

The Individual Search Process

The third study component, the individual search, is quite similar to the research process, although the researcher gets to play Holmes of Baker Street instead of Leakey of Olduvai. The search for an individual involves six important principles: (1) document everything; (2) never leave a lead unresolved; (3) search for consistent behavior patterns; (4) when out of leads, start from the beginning; (5) whenever possible, rely on informal rather than formal sources; and (6) keep the search active to capitalize on chance.

Documenting the Search Process. It is essential to keep a continuous record of every effort made to find an individual: the date on which each lead was pursued, each source contacted, and each question resolved. The accuracy of dating is crucial, for it helps to know how and when to go back to one's search network or to determine how thorough the search has been. Often, additional information on a given research subject becomes available—for example, a correction in the spelling of the person's name or the addition of a birth date. Each of these additions leads to the conclusion that one must return to the original search network to resubmit the name of that person with the additional identifiers. If one is trying to locate a large number of people, it is truly important to know the proper timing of these submissions and how each one relates to the availability of new information. Thorough documentation can prevent one from becoming hopelessly mired in redundant submissions or exhausting organizational helpers, not to mention avoiding tremendous inefficiency of the search. Documentation allows the researcher to go back at any time during the search, in order to pick up exactly where the research left off or to determine whether any lapses have occurred in the search procedure.

Following Through on Leads. Every appointment and every thread must be followed, no matter how inconsequential it may seem. In one case, the absentee owner of a sheltered-care facility was unwilling over the telephone to arrange for a visit to her facility, and we did not follow through on this lead. Approximately one year later, we picked up the documentation of this lack of follow-through, contacted the owner, and discovered that her attitude had changed significantly. As a result, three residents were located.

Another example relates to our efforts to locate an individual who was on the run, protecting herself from members of a cult she believed wished to kill her. Several contacts with legal representatives settling the estate of the cult turned up telephone numbers for this person in an eastern state. We had reason to believe the numbers were those of a relative of the sample member. Ten telephone calls and three letters produced no response, although the phone company listed the numbers as active. Late one night, we made telephone contact with an individual who conveyed a message to our sample member. The sample member called us back from a phone booth. Since she was a former manager of a facility that had closed and could be interviewed on the telephone, she was asked if she wished to participate in such an interview. She gave our secretary the number of the pay phone and indicated she would be available at that phone one time for one half-hour. The telephone call was made, and the interview with this manager completed.

Seeking Patterns of Behavior. Discerning the behavior patterns of sample members can be useful when trying to locate them. It is not uncommon to see patterns of residence change, legal violations, mental health service usage, or criminal justice contacts in a person's behavior. When such a pattern has been discerned, it is often best to wait until the next occurrence of the usual behavior to make contact with the person. For example, for several individuals who are frequent violators of the traffic code, we did a search of Department of Motor Vehicles (DMV) records every other month. Some individuals have had repeated contacts with the criminal justice system (CJS). Thus we stayed in contact regularly with the CJS for any new leads on an individual. One individual with a pattern of traffic violations in

California ran a red light in the state which he had moved. By that point we had already made contact with that out-of-state DMV and were able to locate him because of his consistent behavior pattern.

Starting Over When Leads Are Exhausted. When all leads are exhausted, one must start again. In August of our first search year, we contacted a facility manager for information on a "Dick Duhigg." Finding no record under that name, she could not help us with a lead. We proceeded to use that name in our search network contacts. Four fruitless months later, we again contacted the facility manager. Her secretary rechecked all residents' records. She found none of "Dick" but did find a file on a "Jim Duhigg" whose nickname was "Nick." We presented this new name to a search source who located the county in which Mr. Duhigg was living, approximately 300 miles from his 1973 residence. We made contact with local mental health agencies and eventually spoke with a mental health worker who knew our sample member and would help arrange an interview if Mr. Duhigg was willing. The interview arrangement was complicated because the sample member lived 400 miles from our closest interviewer. We nevertheless made our appointment and followed through with our interview.

Using Informal Rather Than Formal Sources. Table 1 summarizes information on the search process for 70 residents originally interviewed in the San Francisco Bay Area and for 48 in the San Diego area. From our records we compiled the following information for each resident sample member: (1) the time period (in months) elapsed between the date the search began and the date the resident was located and interviewed; (2) the number of different sources contacted during the same time period; and (3) the number of attempted and actual contacts made with these sources during that time period.

The results of our compilation show that our searches for residents in the San Diego area took more time, necessitated contacts with more sources per individual, and necessitated more actual and attempted contacts per source than did our searches in the Bay Area.

Our sources were basically of two kinds. We defined *formal source* as those requiring the principal investigator either to provide a written research protocol and appropriate consent forms or to explain in writing the study's purposes, why we were seeking information, under whose auspices our study was conducted, and other relevant information. All formal sources required, at least initially, a detailed written communication from our study group. *Informal sources* required no such written protocols and explanations; they provided information to us over the telephone or in person. Usually, but not always, informal sources were private individuals—former or current facility managers or residents, mental health professionals, volunteers, relatives, friends, neighbors, telephone operators—whereas formal sources were city, county, state, or federal agencies and departments.

Table 1

Number of months, sources, and contacts per individual search in two search areas

		Bay Area (n = 70)	San Diego (n = 48)	Differences between means
Months	Mean	3.50	4.70	t = − 1.548, p < .10
	Median	2.10	3.25	
	Range	13.30	20.00	
Sources	Means	3.30	5.10	t = − 3.170, p < .01
	Median	2.00	5.00	
	Range	12.00	13.00	
Contacts*	Mean	7.70	12.10	t = − 2.172, p < .05
	Median	4.00	10.50	
	Range	52.00	65.00	

*includes number of attempted and actual contacts.

We added up all sources contacted for all residents in each search area, and categorized them as formal or informal. Table 2 shows the results.

Table 2

Total number and percent of formal and informal sources by search area

| | Bay Area | | San Diego Area | |
	n	%	n	%
Formal	92	39.8	143	58.1
Informal	126	54.6	92	37.4
Unknown	13	5.6	11	4.5
Total	231	100.0	246	100.0

$= 167.978, P < .001$

Table 2 indicates that for the two search areas reported, which involved efforts to locate 118 persons, a minimum of 477 source contacts were necessary. Naturally, a single contact from a single source rarely sufficed to locate a member of our resident sample, unless that person was still living in the same sheltered-care facility as in 1973. In most cases, however, at least two or three contacts or attempted contacts had to be made in order to obtain a lead from—or to give up on—a given information source.

Dealing with formal sources required more efforts than dealing with informal sources. The former had to be contacted more often than informal sources, and took more time to respond to our queries. Contacts and follow-ups with formal sources required extensive documentation, filing, and other clerical duties—which partly explains why our searches in San Diego, where we relied on significantly more formal sources than in the Bay Area (58.1% versus 39.8%, respectively), generally took more time and required more contacts. In the Bay Area, the principal investigator and study group benefitted from an extensive network of informal sources developed over the years. We were able to rely on these to a greater extent than in San Diego, where we had to start, so to speak, from scratch.

If one wished to estimate the costs of conducting searches for hard-to-locate persons, as we have described in this paper, one should expect formal sources to require significantly more staff time and effort, based upon contact requirements. Whenever possible, formal sources should be utilized only after one has exhausted one's informal network.

Capitalizing On Chance. This particular activity is viewed with disdain by most statistically-minded people in the research business. They have noted that many rejections of the null hypothesis are based upon the use of multiple t tests and therefore capitalize on a greater probability of finding a significant result. Still, capitalizing on chance in research remains an important part of the investigative process. Significant discoveries and breakthroughs have resulted from accidents in the laboratory or from having a principal investigator who knows the situation involved in the field so that he or she can observe and make use of chance. This is also true in the investigatory process of locating people.

It helps to have trained people active in the search, for the activity in and of itself creates options for finding people by chance alone, options to capitalize on. In one situation, hoping to find a relative of an individual, we proceeded to call every person with that individual's last name in the county in which that person had lived in 1973. This is a low-yield process that sometimes produces results with people having less common names, such as the individual in question. In one such telephone contact, a woman with the same name as our sample member said she thought she was the only person in the county with that name but that a month ago she had met a woman in her exercise class with the same last name who was the wife of a clergyman. She promised to ask this woman if she knew the index case. A week later the first woman called and told us that in fact our case was the clergyman's son. She conveyed our request to the clergyman to have his son call us collect. The son did call, but he refused to leave a message with our secretary, saying he would call back. When he did not do so within three weeks, we called the original woman, but the exercise class had already ended and our thread of contact was no longer viable. We did learn, however, the city to which the son had moved, giving us the option of calling everyone with the same last name in that area. This we did, and ultimately made contact with and interviewed that individual.

CONCLUSION

Even under the most difficult circumstances, it is possible to complete a longitudinal follow-up study if the research team employs an effective investigatory strategy that includes thorough preplanning and careful adherence to sound procedures. Naturally, success depends on obtaining a high find rate. The successful investigator feels like a Holmes—the unsuccessful one, like a Clouseau.

Research for this paper was supported by the Robert Wood Johnson Foundation, grant #08207, and the National Institute of Mental Health, grant #MH25417. The opinions and conclusions expressed herein are those of the authors and do not necessarily reflect the views of the Robert Wood Johnson Foundation or the National Institute of Mental Health.

REFERENCES

Mednick, S.A. & Baert, A.E. (Eds.). (1981). *Prospective longitudinal research.* Oxford: Oxford University Press.

Schulsinger, F., Mednick, S.A., & Knop, J. (1981). *Longitudinal research, methods, and issues in behavioral science.* Boston: Martinus Nijhoff.

Segal, S.P. & Aviram, A. (1978). *The mentally ill in community-based sheltered care.* New York: John Wiley.

Segal, S.P. & Kaplan, M.S. (1984). One project and twenty-two reviews. *Grants Magazine, 7*(4), 216-224.

Chapter 10
The Role of Foundations in Research on the Chronically Mentally Ill

Carol G. Simonetti

Philanthropic foundations plan an important role in research with the chronically mentally ill. To understand this role, we must first understand how foundations fit into the broader picture of philanthropic giving. Philanthropy in the United States is unique: in 1983 Americans gave $64.93 billion, which is more than $100 million per day. That figure translates into more than $180 for each man, woman, and child. Compare this figure to Canada, where the average contribution is $35 for each person, or to the United Kingdom, where the figure is $20 each.

Who gives all of those dollars? According to the American Association of Fund Raising Counsel (AAFRC), philanthropic giving in the United States broke down as follows:

	$ (billions)	Percentage
Individuals	53.85	82.9
Bequests	4.52	7.0
Foundations	3.46	5.3
Corporations	3.10	4.8
	$64.93	100.0

SOURCE: AAFRC, *Giving U.S.A.* (1984), 7.

It is interesting to note that over half of the individual donations came from people whose family income was less than $20,000 per year.

173

To whom do we give our money? Table 1 illustrates how American philanthropic giving is distributed among several types of organizations.

Table 1

Recipients of All Philanthropy (1983)

Religious organizations and causes	47.8%
Health and hospitals	14.1
Education	13.9
Social welfare	10.7
Arts and humanities	6.3
Civic, housing, environment	2.8
Miscellaneous and foreign	4.4

SOURCE: AAFRC, *Giving U.S.A.* (1984), 7.

This amount of private giving—nearly $65 billion annually—seems like a lot of money, but to put it in perspective we must remember that the federal budget is $932 billion, and state and local government budgets are another $100 billion. The budgets of voluntary organizations are $150 billion, with approximately one-third coming from government, one-third from user fees or tuition, and one-third from contributions. In 1981 an Urban Institute study on the impact of federal budget cuts indicated that for private philanthropy to keep pace with inflation and lost federal revenue, giving would have to increase by 26 percent in 1982, 39 percent in 1983, and 44 percent in 1984. The actual increase, at 10 percent to 14 percent a year, has only been one-third of what is needed.

Foundation giving, which accounts for only 5.3 percent of the total philanthropy, is miniscule compared to either the need or to other funding sources. Yet it can be an important source of funds for several reasons. It can give credibility to a project. It can act as a catalyst for raising other funds or matching support. It is flexible and can respond to new problems or social needs. And foundation giving can also support unpopular causes that government funds cannot.

It is important to know about foundations before approaching them to support your efforts. Without some preliminary research you could be wasting both your time and money. It is estimated that up to 80 percent of requests to foundations are rejected immediately without even a board review. In 1983, for example, The Cleveland Foundation received 831 requests; only 384, or 46 percent, were reviewed by the board, and 110 of those were declined.

TYPES OF FOUNDATIONS

What is a foundation? The Internal Revenue Service defines all 501(c)(3) organizations as private foundations, unless they are explicitly exempt. The IRS then exempts the majority by categorizing them as public charities, churches, schools, and so on. One cannot look at an organization's name and know whether it is a foundation. The Epilepsy Foundation, for example, is a public charity, while the Carnegie Corporation of New York and the Schenley Fund, Inc., are both foundations.

The Foundation Center ascribes the following characteristics to a foundation:

- A nongovernmental, nonprofit organization
- Funds usually from a single source—an individual, family, or corporation
- Programs managed by its own trustees or directors
- Maintains or aids social, educational, charitable, religious, or other activities serving the common welfare
- Primary activity is the making of grants.

Those of us who work in the foundation world have yet a different definition. We think of a foundation as "a body of money surrounded by people who want some."

There are four types of foundations: independent, operating, corporate, and community.

The *independent foundations* are subdivided into three categories.

- *General purpose foundations* operate under broad charters and make grants across a broad spectrum of fields. They have flexibility, at the discretion of their boards of trustees, to allow new program areas. There are approximately 1,000 general purpose foundations that give nationally or regionally, such as Ford, Pew, and Mellon.
- *Special purpose foundations* focus their grantmaking on specific areas usually identified in the will or trust under which they were established or by the interests of the living donors or trustees. This type of foundation, such as the Foundation for Child Development, may be a source of information or publications in its interest area.
- *Family foundations* are the most numerous and the most varied. They are often created by living persons and can serve as vehicles for personal charitable giving, but they can also be very sophisticated organizations run by a professional staff. They may later evolve into special purpose or general purpose foundations.

Operating foundations are a cross between independent foundations and public charities. They spend a majority of their income in the active conduct of their own internal programs, including research and public education in their field of interest, and make few grants to others. An organization of interest to researchers on the chronically mentally ill is the Hogg Foundation for Mental Health, which acts like an Operating Foundation but is, in fact, not a foundation at all but an integral part of the University of Texas. It has, since its inception in 1940, emphasized research and education related to mental health. It controls some restricted funds and grants, totaling over $1 million in 1983, and can make donations only to agencies in Texas.

Corporations support philanthropic efforts through two mechanisms—either directly through the corporation or through a separate *corporate foundation*. The current tax law, as modified in 1981, allows a corporation to give up to 10 percent of its pretax net income; prior to 1981 the limitation had been 5 percent. However, the increase in allowable corporate philanthropy has had little impact: only one-fourth of the country's corporations make any contributions at all, and half of all gifts are made by 1,000 firms. The average giving is 1.05 percent of corporate pretax income. Corporations often favor grants to organizations that are in the community where the firm is located, serve the company's employees, or give the corporation a public relations opportunity. When a firm supports research, it is usually in the field in which the company does business, and it may be needed to improve the company's products.

A *community foundation* differs from an independent foundation in several respects. Its funds come from several sources rather than from a single family or corporation. It does not have some of the burdensome tax regulations because it is, in fact, a public charity under 501(c)(3). A community foundation has a representative board and is usually run by a professional staff. Most important for the mental health researcher, it serves a limited geographic area. The Cleveland Foundation was the founder of the movement in 1914; today there are approximately 300 community foundations.

To whom do these foundations make grants? The breakdown for 1983 is described in Table 2.

Table 2

Recipients of Foundation Grants, 1983

Welfare (civic, social service)	28.4%
Health	21.7
Education	16.0
Cultural	15.4
Science	9.0
Social Science (anthropology, economics, political science)	7.4
Religion	2.1

SOURCE: AAFRC, *Giving U.S.A.* (1984), 7.

Mental health grants are included within several of these fields. The number of grants and the amount of money given specifically for mental health, and their percentage of total foundation giving for 1982 and 1983, are as follows:

	Total Dollars	Percent of Total Fdn Dollars	Total Grants	Percent of Total Fdn Grants
1982	$16,493,486	1.1	503	1.9
1983	25,162,308	1.4	559	1.7

SOURCE: AAFRC, *Giving U.S.A.* (1984), 22.

These are the total dollars and grants in the mental health field. Research with the chronically mentally ill is, of course, only a part of the total research in mental health.

FINDING AND WINNING GRANTS

It is impossible to identify trends of foundation funding in research for the chronically mentally ill. There are no trends in what foundations as a whole support. There may, however, be trends within individual foundations, and this is what you need to find out. The only way to determine a foundation's trend is to look at its history, since foundations do not usually project future giving patterns. To determine which foundations you should approach, you should start by identifying all possible foundations, single out the most appropriate, then list them according to the best possible match. You need to believe in your project and then find a like-minded foundation. Apply criteria of geography, interest area, similar grantees, methodology, client groups served, types of support, and sizes of grants.

Sources: The Foundation Center

Fortunately, there is a source for all the information you need—the Foundation Center, in New York, which is the only not-for-profit corporation in the United States dedicated to the collection, analysis, and dissemination of information on philanthropic foundations. The Center maintains a branch office in Washington, D.C., and field offices in San Francisco and Cleveland. It also has over 160 cooperative library collections, with at least one in every state.

The Foundation publishes the *National Data Book,* which lists information on all currently active U.S. grantmaking private foundations, including the name, address, contact person, asset size, and total grants authorized. The book's limitation is that it has no subject information, and it may not be a particularly helpful source since there are almost 22,000 foundations listed but only about 10 percent have assets over $1 million or make grants of $100,000 or more. These foundations can be found in the *Foundation Directory,* which includes approximately 4,000 foundations representing 90 percent of all foundation assets and 80 percent of all foundation giving. The *Directory* includes the name, address, telephone number, all officers and directors, the donors, a purpose statement, the assets and total grants, the largest and smallest grants and brief application information.

Finding the Best Foundation: A Simulation

To prepare this paper, I examined foundation support of research in mental health. My first step was to look at the field-of-interest index in the *Foundation Directory.* The key is to be creative, and I identified 28 possible fields:

Aged	Medical education
Alcoholism	Medical sciences
Biochemistry	Mental health
Buildings and equipment	Nutrition
Chemistry	Pharmacy
Child development	Physical sciences
Child Welfare	Psychiatry
Drug abuse	Psychology
Education	Rehabilitation
Educational research	Scholarships
Family services	Science and technology
Handicapped	Social services
Health	Women
Higher education	Youth

This is not an exhaustive list. You might identify others depending on the nature of your project.

I then took the single category of mental health and looked at those foundations that make grants nationally. (You would also want to look at your own state.) In the 1983 edition I found 20 foundations. In the supplement there were 12 foundations with updated information, but these were all in my 1983 list. I further narrowed the list of 20 to the nine that seemed to have the strongest interest in mental health research. The others specifically indicated they had no interest in research or, like the Stone Foundation in Illinois, indicated its funds were presently committed and they were accepting no new applications. Of the nine, some were more appropriate than others; for example, The Joseph P. Kennedy, Jr. Foundation is more interested in research on mental retardation than on the chronically mentally ill. The *Directory* provided summaries on each foundation. Following is the description of the MacArthur Foundation:

MacArthur (John D. and Catherine T.) Foundation
140 South Dearborn Street
Chicago, IL 60603   (312) 726-8000

Incorporated in 1970 in Illinois
Donor(s): John D. MacArthur

Purpose and Activities: Broad purposes; four major initiatives currently authorized: MacArthur Fellows Program, for highly talented individuals in any field of endeavor (self-initiated or outside nominations not considered); the Health Program, primarily for research in mental health and the psychological and behavioral aspects of health and rehabilitation; the General Grants Program, primarily for education, governance, public affairs, civil and criminal justice, and mass communication; and the Special Grants Program, for support of cultural and community activities in the Chicago metropolitan area. No grants for capital or endowment funds, propaganda, lobbying efforts, political activities or campaigns, conferences, publications, films, debt retirement, development campaigns, fundraising appeals, churches, or scholarships and fellowships (except MacArthur Fellows Program which is foundation-initiated); no loans. In future years, almost all of the foundation's grants will be initiated by the board of directors.

Financial Data (Yr. ended 12/31/81): Assets, $927,967,952 (M);

gifts received, $12,500; expenditures, $44,073,530, including $31,818,060 for 236 grants (high: $1,200,000; low: $2,500).

Officers: Paul D. Doolen, Chairman; William T. Kirby, Vice-Chairman and Secretary; John E. Corbally, President; James M. Furman, Executive Vice-President; Joseph A. Diana, Vice-President for Administration and Treasurer; William Bevan, Vice-President and Director of Health Program; Gerald Freund, Vice-President and Director of MacArthur Fellows Program; David M. Murdock, Vice-President, Finance.

Directors: Robert P. Ewing, Gaylord Freeman, Murray Gell-Mann, Paul Harvey, Edward H. Levi, J. Roderick MacArthur, Jonas Salk, M.D., Jerome B. Weisner.

Write: James M. Furman, Executive Vice-President.

Grant Application Information: Program policy statement and grant application guidelines available; initial approach by letter; submit one copy of proposal, direct applications for Prize Fellows Program not accepted; board meets monthly, except August.

The next source I explored was the *Grants Index,* which lists grants of $5,000 or more by 450 major foundations, including the 100 largest. These foundations account for 60 percent of all assets and 50 percent of all grants made. The index includes the foundation name and address and any limitation statement. The grant information includes the recipient, location, grant amount, duration, and purpose. Again, you should be creative when scanning the index. By the time I was partially through the H's in the index, I had listed 52 topics. Under the topic of mental health research, I found 20 grants. However, seven of those grants were from different foundations in the amount of $5,000 or $10,000 to support a capital campaign at the Menninger Foundation. Following is information I gleaned on 11 grants that seemed most relevant. Eight of the 11 were from the John D. and Catherine T. MacArthur Foundation, and four of these grants were for developing networks devoted to interdisplinary research.

MacArthur (John D. and Catherine T.) Fdn.
       8960. Determinants and Consequences of Health-Promoting and Health-Damaging Behavior Network, Chicago, IL. $805,000, 1982 for creation of research network to facilitate progress in this

critical area of mental health research. This MacArthur Mental Health Research Network is composed of research groups at the following institutions: Duke University Medical Center, Karolinska Institutet (Sweden), University of California at Los Angeles, University of California at San Francisco, University of Pennsylvania and Yale University. 1982 AR.

8977. Illinois State Psychiatric Institute, Chicago, IL. $81,818, 1982. 3-year grant to compare two models of sex differences in schizophrenia, in order to understand and refine diagnostic system and sub-type classifications.

8978. Illinois State Psychiatric Institute, Chicago, IL. $42,850, 1982. 2-year grant to examine relationship between electrophysiological, biochemical and behavioral measures in schizophrenic patients. 1982 AR.

9003. National Academy of Sciences, D.C. $20,000, 1982. For use by Institute of Medicine, to study impact of governmental policies on mental health research and mental health services. 1982 AR.

9015. Psychobiology of Depression and Other Affective Disorders Network, Chicago, IL. $105,000, 1982. For creation of research network to facilitate progress in this critical area of mental health research. This MacArthur Mental Health Network is composed of research groups at the following institutions: McLean Hospital (Belmont, MA), Salk Institute for Biological Studies, Stanford University, University of Illinois and University of Pittsburgh. 1982 AR.

9018. Risk and Protective Factors in Major Mental Health Disorders Network, Chicago, IL. $805,000, 1982. For creation of research network to facilitate progress in this critical area of mental health research. This MacArthur Mental Health Research Network is composed of research groups at the following institutions: Institute of Psychiatry (London), University of California at Irvine, University of California at Los Angeles, Washington University in Saint Louis, and Yale University. 1982 AR.

9021. Stanford University, Stanford, CA. $295,306, 1982. 3-year grant. To develop measures of environmental stressors, resources and coping responses and to improve understanding of development of physical and psychological illness. 1982 AR.

9024. Transition from Infancy to Early Childhood Network, Chicago, IL. $797,000, 1982. For creation of research network to facilitate progress in this critical area of mental health research. This MacArthur Mental Health Research Network is composed of research groups at the following institutions: Harvard Univer-

sity, Foundation for Advanced Education in the Sciences, Inc.—
on behalf of the National Institute of Mental Health, University
of California at San Diego, University of Colorado Health
Sciences Center, and University of Washington. 1982 AR.

Grant (William T.) Foundation
19280. University of Newcastle Upon Tyne, Medical School,
Newcastle Upon Tyne, England. $5,000, 2/25/82. For interim
support for the Three Generational Study of the Transmission of
Deprivation. 12/20/82 FF.

Pittsburgh Foundation
29165. University of Pittsburgh, Medical School, Pittsburgh, PA
$5,792, 2/23/83. For research in neurophysiobiology mental
disorders. 3/23/83 GL.

Scaife (Sarah) Foundation
LM: Grants primarily for public policy programs that address
major domestic and international issues; additional areas of interest primarily in the western PA area. No grants to individuals.

29198. American Institutes for Research in the Behavioral
Sciences, Cambridge, MA. $114,200, 1982. For study, Psychiatry
and the Free Society. 1982 AR.

You would want to update this information by looking at the
bimonthly updates.

As a companion to the *Foundation Grants Index,* the Foundation Center publishes *Comsearch* printouts, which list grants
by program areas and selected geographic areas. Unfortunately,
the one for mental health, which in 1984 included 412 grants for
over $23 million from 164 foundations, specifically excludes
psychological or behavioral research.

The Foundation Center will do a computer search for current
information on grants. This is usually discouraged, since the information is expensive and is often superficial. Nevertheless, I
decided to try it and requested information. I focused on grants
made since 1984, including both mental health and research.
The computer listed 51 grants, but all except 11 were from the
same foundation, the William T. Grant Foundation, which I
had already identified. The price was $30 to find this out.

Now, with several foundations on which I would like more
in-depth information, I would look in the *Source Book Profile,*
which gives comprehensive information on about a thousand of

the largest independent, community, and corporate foundations. This information is updated periodically. From it I can learn a lot about the MacArthur Foundation and its interest in mental health research, including the important information that it does not accept direct applications for its Health Program grants, including the Networks, but that almost $800,000 has been set aside for future mental health grants.

I can get still more information on the MacArthur Foundation by reviewing its annual report, since it is one of about six hundred foundations that publish one, and by looking at its IRS tax form 990 PF, which is available through the Foundation Center or the Internal Revenue Service. Other sources are the *Taft Foundation Reporter,* which gives a brief biography on the trustees of major foundations as well as information on grants, and the *Foundation News,* which is a bimonthly magazine published by the Council on Foundations and includes current issues in grant making.

Winning A Grant

The secret to winning grants is not to look for overall trends but to find a foundation interested in supporting what you believe is important. Does your project fit the mission of that foundation? Are you in its geographic area of giving? Does it support research? Have they given to organizations similar to yours? Is the size of your request within their scope?

When you have identified a foundation or foundations with which you believe there is a good fit, you must then let the foundation know you exist, what you are doing, and why they should be interested in funding you. This is usually done via a proposal. One way to show that you have done your homework in targeting their foundation is to follow their published guidelines. If the foundation prefers a letter of inquiry first, send one; if it limits the size of proposals, limit yours. If it requires certain signatures on the cover letter, be sure to get them.

Many foundations do not have staff to meet with grantees, so your proposal must speak for you. There are many excellent books on proposal writing, available through the Foundation

Center as well as in most public libraries. Do not be concerned if you are not a professional proposal writer. Foundations are looking for content over style. Your proposal should be clear, concise, and free of jargon. In case you do not have the opportunity to present your case orally, your proposal should answer as many questions as possible. When in doubt about the direct relevancy of information, include it as an addendum. The proposal should answer *who, what, why, when, where,* and *how much it will cost; who you are, what you are planning to do, why you want to do it, when you will do it, where you will do it;* and a *complete realistic budget.* And your proposal should show how your goals fit the goals and objectives of the foundation.

Remember that the problem you want to address may be the most important in the world to you, but so is everyone else's who submits a proposal. Your work alone will not solve the problems of the world, so be realistic about what the foundation's support would enable you to do. This will go a long way toward another key question a foundation will ask—your ability to accomplish your goals and objectives.

Does who you know count? No one can say that it does not help to know key decision makers and that it would be foolish not to use available networks. Support letters, especially from groups who would benefit from your services and from other groups or individuals willing to commit their resources to your success, are also helpful. But look at a list of agencies that foundations do fund and you will see many grassroot groups without connections. Foundations want to fund good projects, ones that will succeed, not just those run by people who "know someone."

POSTSCRIPT

Winning a research grant takes a lot of work and only you can decide if your project is worth it. But remember, foundations' sole purpose for existing is to fund worthwhile efforts to solve problems and seize opportunities to create a better society for us all. "All" includes the chronically mentally ill.

PART III: CONCLUSION

Chapter 11

The Chronically Mentally Ill and Social-Problem Research

Stuart A. Kirk

The chronically mentally ill have only recently become a focus of sustained public attention. They are a second generation concern, the offspring of a concern expressed in 1961 by the National Joint Commission on Mental Illness and Health in its final report to the U.S. Congress (Joint Commission, 1961). The report recommended that those with "major mental illness" be helped to maintain themselves in the community and to overcome "the debilitating effects of institutionalization as much as possible" (Joint Commission, 1961, p. xvii). The Joint Commission recognized that there was a need for services for the chronically mentally ill, and it suggested that large state mental hospitals be gradually converted into centers for long-term care of all chronic diseases, including mental illness.

Mental health reformers in the 1960s were aware of the iatrogenic effects of institutionalization and responded to the need for community care, but there was little recognition of the need for prolonged care. In the ensuing reforms that produced community mental health, those in need of prolonged care were largely ignored—only to emerge ten years later as the "chronically mentally ill," an underserved population that was a victim of the unintentional oversight of earlier reforms (Segal & Baumohl, 1982).

The papers in this volume recognize these developments and seek to shed light on the related research problems. The research issues cannot be separated from conceptual work, nor can they be fully understood outside the social context in which the chronically mentally ill have emerged as a social problem. This final paper will trace how research has developed in parallel with the emergence of the chronically mentally ill as a social problem. Many of the conceptual and methodological problems facing researchers stem from the relatively recent discovery of this population.

THE DISCOVERY OF SOCIAL PROBLEMS

During the winter of 1974, the United States experienced a sudden, widespread problem that came to be called the "energy crisis." The media carried daily stories of the crisis, the topic was a matter of constant discussion among citizens, the federal government initiated immediate measures, and the daily routines of millions of Americans were disrupted as gasoline became difficult to find and expensive to buy. By the following summer, however, the media rarely carried such news, the topic was rarely the subject of conversation, our driving habits were back to normal, and there was even some evidence of a surplus of gasoline. In the space of a few months, we experienced the making, then the dissolution, of a social crisis. Our experience of the energy crisis is noteworthy because it illustrates how social problems rise and decline.

How do social crises—whether energy, delinquency, or homelessness—come into our national consciousness? By what processes do we begin to recognize political corruption, spouse abuse, AIDS, or cigarette smoking as worthy of serious concern? Social problems tend to emerge and then disappear. The use of marijuana, for example, has gone, in the course of two decades, from being viewed as socially dangerous to being seen as less threatening. The consumption of alcohol, similarly, has been viewed quite differently during different periods of recent history (Gusfield, 1963; 1981). Even cigarette smoking, which was completely banned in 14 states at the turn of the century, became a legal and even an encouraged behavior before the recent turn toward government regulation and growing opposition by nonsmokers (Nuehring & Markle, 1974).

But why do some social conditions or behaviors become defined as "problems" and not others? An easy answer might be that the most serious problems draw our most serious attention, but that is not always so. Poverty existed in the United States long before it was "discovered" by Michael Harrington and described in *The Other America* (1962). Racism, too, was prevalent long before the urban riots of the 1960s forced it to the nation's attention. Sex discrimination is now recognized as a serious problem, although it is neither new nor increasing. And no one has demonstrated that chronic mental illness is now more widespread than previously. How, then, have the chronically mentally ill become the subject of research, social policy initiatives, and national conferences?

The Emergence of Social Problems

Social conditions come to be seen as problematic through a complex process of collective definition (Blumer, 1971). At each stage, critical decisions are made that determine both the nature of the problem and its development.

In the *pre-problem* stage, phenomena are not recognized by the society as problematic. Private individuals or special interest groups may recognize, define, and focus on the condition and call it a problem, but only under certain circumstances can they advance their problem definition so that it receives attention and consideration by a wider audience of opinion makers—leading politicians, foundations, and the heads of government agencies.

Prior to the late 1960s, the chronically mentally ill were not a serious concern of the public or even of the mental health profession. No major demographic research was conducted, no special programs were funded, no new training programs were designed to prepare professionals to work with them. The concern expressed by the Joint Commission (1961) was about the pernicious effects of institutionalization and the lack of services in the community for ambulatory patients. The Commission's recommendation to expand services to the acutely ill was expected to prevent chronicity. The few mentally ill who did not respond to these rehabilitative efforts were to be treated in chronic-disease hospitals. Chronic mental illness was expected to disappear either as a result of effective community treatment or as a result of being treated in chronic-disease hospitals. No one in 1961 predicted that it would emerge as a specific social problem by the end of the decade.

Some pre-problem social conditions never advance into prominence, and remain forever a problem for a few rather than an active concern for many. Champions of pre-problem social conditions may work tirelessly to convince others of the condition's gravity or wait for circumstances to change dramatically for the worse so the condition achieves the attention they feel it deserves.

In the *emergence* stage, the situation is recognized by more than the individuals or interest groups who had been lobbying for the problem. The emergence of the problem may be due to several factors: a dramatic event or crisis; a public revelation concerning the problem achieved through newspaper reporting; a dramatic worsening of the condition; the discovery of harmfulness through scientific research; or personal experience with the problem by a prominent person. All these possibilities rely to some extent on the coverage given the problem by radio, television, news magazines and newspapers.

By 1970 the development of community mental health centers throughout the country had drastically altered the profile of mental health services. The population in residence at state mental hospitals had been steadily declining through a combination of factors including the discharge of former long-term patients, shorter stays for those newly admitted, and more stringent admissions criteria. Simultaneously, community mental health facilities began providing services to new populations not being served by the state hospitals.

But local newspapers began to print stories on the fate of patients who had been discharged from state hospitals. While the term "chronically mentally ill" had not yet become the official problem label, the rapid rise of the new concept of "deinstitutionalization," initially coined to promote the philosophy of community care, slowly took on the connotation of an emerging social problem. Local media, particularly those in communities near state hospitals that were reducing their resident population, ran stories about the concentration of former patients in particular neighborhoods, zoning battles involving local residents attempting to keep neighborhoods free from board-and-care facilities for the mentally ill, and about the increasing involvement of the police in the control of those heretofore under the jurisdiction of state mental health authorities.

It was only after the emergence of "deinstitutionalization" as a problem, rather than as a solution, that researchers turned their attention to describing and interpreting the nature of this developing problem (Bachrach, 1976; Kirk & Therrien, 1975). A flood of research followed, describing the problem and subtly shifting the conceptual focus from the process of depopulating state mental hospitals to the fate of former patients. Thus the problem of deinstitutionalization, which could have been defined as structural disabilities between state and federal government, between state hospitals and community mental health centers, or between health care and social welfare programs, came instead to be defined as the personal disabilities of troubled people. This shift of attention has had a profound effect on subsequent research on the chronically mentally ill.

Problem Legitimization and Mobilization

Many social conditions receive temporary public attention but never become defined as social problems. Public recognition of a problematic condition does not lead automatically to problem *legitimization* (Blumer, 1971). Problems will not be legitimized unless key leaders—newspaper editors, members of important foundations, political party officials, heads of government agencies, and powerful special interest groups—become concerned and begin to discuss it. This initial discussion often has the quality of "alarmed discovery" (Downs, 1972), in which references are made to the injustice or danger that the condition poses to the nation's values, traditions, and future. When such claims are made, especially by high-ranking officials, it is a clear sign that a social problem has been recognized and major research projects are being launched.

Such alarm about the chronically mentally ill was first voiced by several important studies in the 1970s. The first was Ralph Nader's study of community mental health centers, which focused on the gap between their promise and their product, particularly with regard to the seriously mentally ill (Chu & Trotter, 1974). Whatever skepticism greeted the Nader report was erased shortly afterward by a federal government study (Comptroller General, 1977) which showed that community mental health centers were inadequately serving those released from state hospitals. At the same time, professional mental health journals began publishing articles describing and analyzing the problem. In only ten years, "deinstitutionalization" had gone from the rally cry of professional reformers to a label for the unintended consequences of ill-planned social intervention.

When Jimmy Carter appointed the President's Commission on Mental Health in 1977, few doubted that the various shortcomings of the mental health system would become a focus of concern. The Commission's final report (President's Commission, 1978) used as its theme "the underserved," giving prominent feature to the chronically mentally ill, who had been finally recognized and approved as a legitimate social problem.

Once a problem is legitimized, there is usually a flurry of enthusiasm for solving it quickly—people are ready for *mobilization*. Before rational action is taken, however, a systematic understanding of the problem may be sought. During this stage, conflicting analyses and alternative solutions are studied. For example, when recognition and concern arose about poverty, there was extensive debate over its causes and solutions (Aaron, 1978). Was poverty due to the culture of the poor or to the structure of economic opportunities available in the society? Proposals were advanced by various groups, and solutions to the problem were widely debated. Solutions to problems vary in cost and the extent to which they would require major readjustments in social institutions. The willingness of those in power to pay the price to solve the problem is tested. At this juncture the problem runs the risk of being abandoned and returned to the pre-problem stage. But if the will to alleviate the problem remains, a *plan of action* is developed.

The report of the President's Commission on Mental Health (1978) was such a product. It contained general recommendations on mental health issues ranging from prevention to personnel, including some proposals specifically for the chronically mentally ill. Within months these general recommendations were taken up by an interagency task force, which produced an implementation plan calling for new federal legislation. This report led quickly to the introduction and passage by Congress in October 1980 of the Mental Health Systems Act (PL 96-398) and the development of a detailed HEW report "National Plan for the Chronically Mentally Ill" (August, 1980) that included specific steps required for financing care.

After official policy is made, programs are developed, staff recruited and trained, administrative machinery developed and placed in working order, potential clients contacted and informed of the new programs, links with existing programs and agencies forged, and so on. This is the *implementation* stage. In this process of putting the official plan into operation, the redefinition of the social problem can, and often does, take place. Administrators often begin to substitute their proposals for those intended in the official legislation, opponents of the official plan work to restrict or undercut its implementation, and those who stand to gain from the official plan attempt to usurp as much power and influence as possible during the implementation stage.

The detailed plans and legislation signed by President Carter that emerged out of the President's Commission between 1978 and 1980 never reached the implementation stage. In 1980 the election of President Reagan and the passage of block grant legislation effectively repealed the Mental Health Systems Act and with it most of the action plans to provide comprehensive services to the chronically mentally ill or other underserved populations.

Even after an official plan has been implemented but before anything like a problem resolution is obtained, popular interest in the problem may decline, funding for programs and research may be cut, and the official plan may be scrapped, divided among other existing agencies of government, or left to struggle ineffectively with its original task. The War on Poverty and Model Cities programs reached this final stage, in which they slowly disappeared, and the problems they were meant to solve fell back to the pre-problem stage, awaiting reincarnation.

When official attention is not given to a problem, it may reemerge in whole or part as another problem. The National Plan for the Chronically Mentally Ill was announced in August, 1980. Its demise began shortly after, when a series of other phenomena began clamoring for national attention in the media, much like deinstitutionalization had a decade earlier: homelessness among adults, youth vagrancy, multiple substance abuse, and sexual and economic exploitation of the mentally disabled. These new urban ills had woven through them the implication that they are traceable partially to the depopulation of state hospitals. Many new research agenda have been spawned by this development, and they are touched on by some of the papers in this volume. These new foci for research should be viewed as a natural evolution and differentiation of research on the chronically mentally ill even if the populations and issues are distinctly different. As with all good social problem research, careful analysis often eventually leads to the recognition of a web of interacting problems.

RESEARCH ISSUES AND THE CHRONICALLY MENTALLY ILL

It is easy to demonstrate the cyclical nature of social problems either by focusing on those conditions that were once a great concern of the society or by mentioning conditions which have recently emerged as new problems even though there is no evidence that they are more prevalent than before. Such "new" problems as adolescent suicide, spouse abuse, sexual abuse of children, homelessness, or the chronically mentally ill serve as illustrations. The social problem cycle, however, shapes more than the opinions of the citizens and political decision makers. It also influences the character of the research and problem analysis that is done on these conditions. As a problem emerges and becomes the target of formal action plans, there is an interactive process in which social researchers play a significant role, the actual nature of which is itself the subject of study and debate. Social research is shaped by and shapes the social problem cycle. There are occasions where research results are influential in identifying a problem, suggesting its causes, documenting its effects, and mapping a plan of action. (This is when social scientists congratulate themselves for providing leadership in the policy making process.) But there are at least as many times, as Henry Aaron (1978) has suggested, when social science seems to come after, rather than before, changes in policy.

The development of research on the chronically mentally ill is similar to research on other social problems. As we have already described, research has influenced the way the chronically mentally ill have become defined as a problem. A series of early studies cautioned against the debilitating effects of long-term hospitalization (Goffman, 1961). This was reinforced by others who suggested psychiatric labeling had self-fulfilling tendencies (Scheff, 1966). Several studies offered evidence that psychoactive drugs and community services were effective alternatives to hospitalization (Hogarty et al., 1973). Evaluation studies helped to document the fate of former patients and the extent to which they became connected to community mental health programs (Kirk, 1976). And researchers helped shift the problem definition from deinstitutionalization to the chronically mentally ill. In this context, the evolution of research on the chronically mentally ill can be examined in relation to both the conceptual and methodological problems it encounters. These problems are discussed in many of the papers in this volume.

Conceptual Issues

Concepts are convenient tools for summarizing collections of observations. They provide us with a common language for discourse, and by doing so increase our sense of understanding and control. But concepts can also be reified, distorting our thinking, capturing realities that don't exist and lulling us into a false sense of enlightenment. This certainly is evident in the evolution of thinking about mental disorder. Bachrach, in chapter 2, describes the evolution of mental health conceptualization as "chronic progressive fuzziness" in critically analyzing such concepts as "community support systems."

Throughout this book other authors raise questions about some of our most commonly used concepts. A few will serve as examples of the conceptual problems confronting those doing research in this evolving area.

Chronic mental illness has emerged as one of those new concepts that can mislead as it attempts to clarify. Goldman et al. (1981) define the term in relation to three criteria: diagnosis, disability, and duration. The chronically mentally ill are people with particular psychiatric diagnoses, who are limited in daily living skills, and whose disorders persist for long periods of time. While appearing to draw a tight circle around a group of similar people—labeled the chronically mentally ill—the elements of the definition weaken upon close examination.

Chronicity. The notion of "chronicity" bears a special burden. It purports to distinguish this particular problem population from others with mental disorders. Traditionally, those patients who had long stays in state hospitals were defined as "chronics." Since long stays were the norm prior to the 1950s, there was an easily identified group that qualified for the designation "chronically mentally ill." Questions of diagnosis, etiology, or treatment could remain cloudy; chronics were simply those found inside state asylums. It was conceptually and empirically tidy.

Using duration of hospital stay to define chronicity has become problematic since the role of state hospitals has changed. Fewer patients stay long; some move to nursing homes; some are treated periodically by community hospitals and clinics; others stay beyond the reach of any psychiatric services. Consequently, defining chronicity only in relation to length of hospitalization is now inadequate. We now recognize that length of treatment or hospitalization is at least as much a function of organizational and policy decisions as it is of a patient's need.

In place of long hospital stays, we now find frequent references to the "new chronics," those we assume would have been suitable candidates for long-term hospitalization had they lived before the era of deinstitutionalization. New chronics may never have been admitted to a psychiatric facility, although there may be evidence of serious and lengthy disabilities.

Moreover, late adolescents without the opportunity to establish a lengthy record of troubles are described as the "young adult chronically mentally ill."

A definition of chronicity, released from its mooring in hospital stays, is now in search of new empirical grounding. "New chronics" or "young adult chronics" suggest a predictive validity that few psychiatric concepts enjoy. Chronicity, like homelessness, poverty, or unemployment, may reflect a temporary rather than a permanent condition. This is suggested by both Moxley in chapter 4 and by the longitudinal research of Harding (1985). The warning to researchers is not to confuse a problem with a self-fulfilling prophecy.

Disability. As the traditional measures of chronicity are invalidated, the concepts we use to describe dysfunction take on more crucial importance. Traditional diagnostic categories have limited utility because their descriptions of functional behavior are unreliable and lack relevance. In place of psychiatric diagnosis, researchers have attempted to describe individuals in terms of their abilities and disabilities. Disabled persons are viewed as those who have deficits or impairments that make them more "dependent" than "normals." And since independence is greatly valued in our culture, dependents are stigmatized as Wikler describes in chapter 5. This traditional concept of disability can be faulted on both conceptual and empirical grounds.

Empirically, disability is not unidimensional, with the independent and the dependent at opposite poles. Everyone is dependent and independent simultaneously, in relation to different capacities, different environmental demands and different time periods. Coulton, in chapter 7, suggests that independence for the mentally ill may not be bipolar.

Locating disability in a person overlooks the fact that disability is usually a function of the interaction between individual capacities and environmental demands and of the availability of mechanisms for mediating these two (Coulton, chapter 7). Environmental and technological innovations can often do as much to overcome disabilities as efforts directed primarily toward a person. For example, hearing aids, eye glasses, and even automobiles provide abilities where there is incapacity.

Furthermore, our conceptualization of the environment is too often defined by geographical location (e.g., "in the community") or physical structure (e.g., "institutional care") without adequate attention to other aspects of a person's environment. Certainly the physical structure and geographical location are important aspects of the environment. But equally important and conceptually distinct are the demands and supports (both perceived and real) that emanate from family and friends, neighbors and strangers, supervisors and co-workers. Finally, and perhaps most importantly, concepts of disability need to connect individual capacities and characteristics of the environment. One of our more fruitful conceptual areas may lie in understanding the fit between the person and the environment.

As the chronically mentally ill have emerged as a serious social concern, our conceptualizations have evolved from simple, almost stereotypical descriptions to a greater appreciation of the limits of the concepts. A critical review of terms like chronicity, disability, and environment is more likely to lead to conceptual clarity, productive research, and more effective service programs.

Methodological Issues

The evolution of research on social problems parallels their emergence in public consciousness. As problems arise and gain attention, the initial research often consists primarily of journalistic accounts and anecdotes, expert opinion without the benefit of specific knowledge of the particular problem, simple "guesstimates," and crude counting of the number of people afflicted. In the initial stages, government agencies usually will not have collected or organized data in a way that specifically pertains to the new target population, so there is considerable extrapolation from existing data sets. Anyone who already has done some research, no matter how limited, on the emerging problem may be plucked from obscurity by the national media and be conferred with the status of expert. Nonrandom and unsystematic surveys of limited segments of the target population will be squeezed for national generalizations. As a result of this attention and the recognition of the limits of available knowledge, new studies will be funded by foundations, and government agencies will request proposals. These new inquiries stimulate both better conceptualizations of the problem and more methodologically sophisticated research (Aaron, 1978).

This evolution in research sophistication can be seen in studies of delinquency, spouse and child abuse, substance abuse, and acquired immune deficiency syndrome (AIDS). And it can be seen in research on the chronically mentally ill presented in the papers in this volume.

Research on the chronically mentally ill has advanced far beyond the state of initial, unsystematic reports and expert opinion. As Allen Rubin illustrates in chapter 1, there is now an informative literature available, much of it developed by sound research procedures. Nevertheless, research on the chronically mentally ill is not without its deficiencies, due both to the relatively recent emergence of the problems and to some particular aspect of the phenomena. Some of the major methodological issues pertain to the instability of the target population, internal and external validity of intervention research, and access to reliable information.

Instability of the population refers to both the definitional ambiguities of who is chronically mentally ill as well as to the actual circumstances of their lives. On the conceptual level, as Rubin in chapter 1, and Bachrach in chapter 2, point out, inconsistent or inadequate definitions of the chronically mentally ill cannot only muddle a particular study but can also impede the accumulation of knowledge. Instability of circumstances refers to the frequently cited problem of identifying and tracking this population. There are many who have suggested that the chronicaly mentally ill are geographically mobile and difficult to track in follow-up studies. (See Segal and Cohen, chapter 9, and Bachrach, chapter 2.) But in addition to their residential mobility, the chronically mentally ill have fluctuating levels of functioning, making them not readily identifiable in cross-sectional studies. This combination of residential mobility and level of functioning makes the chronically mentally ill often indistinguishable from other populations of concern, e.g., the homeless or substance abusers.

Allen Rubin points out that research on the effectiveness of services for the chronically mentally ill is limited by some particular threats to internal and external validity. Although one can find examples in the literature of just about any research inadequacy, several appear to be more common to this population. In evaluation research, selection and control of treatment groups is a common issue. Unlike college sophomores who can be expected to participate dutifully in the experiments of their faculty, transient clients on the margins of society have few incentives to cooperate. Moreover, special research/demonstration projects, which must rely on homogeneity of subjects for design and statistical reasons and on voluntary participation for ethical, legal, and practical reasons, always run the risk of sacrificing population generalizability for experimental control. Furthermore, as Rubin and Solomon point out, many studies that have attempted to collect follow-up data on treatment and control groups encounter serious problems of attrition in samples. The recent longitudinal studies by Harding (1985) and Segal, reported in chapter 9, overcame this problem only by unique circumstances and heroic efforts, illustrating the seriousness of the problem.

Much of the treatment research is also limited by the failure to specify the nature of the intervention. In part, this is a problem of failure to make operational such concepts as community treatment, support networks, rehabilitation, and family counseling. But it is also the inevitable result of the fact that the chronically mentally ill require, and frequently receive, many types of help from different service providers. The problems caused by multiple treatments of an unspecified nature when each has intended as well as unintended effects present a formidable challenge to even the best data analyst.

Finally, gaining access to relevant and reliable data requires interpersonal, political, and organizational skills, and patience of the first order (see Solomon's chapter). Talk with anyone who has conducted research on the chronically mentally ill, and you hear similar stories of sloppy, incomplete, and inaccurate agency records; disinterested, suspicious or overworked staff;

cautious, retentive, and paranoid agency executives; and the need to make research compromises to keep the study alive.

CONCLUSION

Although the chronically mentally ill have emerged only recently as a serious concern and research on them is complex, we have learned a great deal. It is a sure sign of growing maturity when researchers become aware of what is unknown but knowable. The papers in this volume suggest three directions for future research to pursue the knowable. The first direction, suggested by the work of Coulton, Spaniol, Wikler and others, calls for a focus on the person-environment interaction of the chronically mentally ill, including institutional environments as well as the important environments provided by families and social networks. The second direction, and a common one as social problem research progresses, is toward longitudinal studies such as those suggested by the work of Wikler and Segal and, on a clinical scale, by Jayaratne. The third direction is toward more and better synthetic efforts to cull from existing studies trends and guidelines for practice.

In addition, the papers suggest a need for theory development, more by the relative absence than the presence of such discussion. Early theorizing proved inadequate for understanding the chronically mentally ill. Psychoanalytical formulations did not provide a useful framework for research or service programs. Similarly, sociological theories emphasizing labeling and social-role performance were unable to provide much help. Perhaps this accounts for the largely atheoretical and empirical approach that characterizes much of the current research. The emphasis is now adequate definitions (Goldman et al., 1985), conceptual clarity (Bachrach), longitudinal description (Solomon, Segal) and intervention effectiveness (Rubin, Spaniol, Moxley). At present, questions about etiology or social functions are relatively absent. Perhaps this also is characteristic of a particular stage of social problem research.

If a social problem comes into prominence and remains a focus of concern for an extended period, both the conceptual issues and the character of the research will evolve from initial simplicity to a challenging complexity. Concepts such as the chronically mentally ill that once served to identify and highlight a particular social concern later appear to obscure and distort the phenomena. Research methodologies that produce the first systematic description of the problem are eventually replaced by more rigorous and refined procedures. The paradoxical result of this evolution is that the more we learn, the more tentative and guarded are our conclusions (Aaron, 1978). Conceptual and research sophistication complicate the work of social intervention, but that is the price of progress and knowledge.

REFERENCES

Aaron, H.J. (1978). *Politics and the professors.* Washington, D.C.: The Brookings Institution.

Bachrach, L. (1976). *Deinstitutionalization: An analytic review and sociological perspective.* DHEW, 76-351. Washington, D.C.: U.S. Government Printing Office.

Blumer, H. (1971). Social problems as collective behavior. *Social Problems, 18*(3), 298-306.

Chu, F.D. & Trotter, S. (1974). *The madness establishment.* New York: Grossman.

Comptroller General of the United States (1977). Report to the Congress, January 7, 1977. *Returning the mentally disabled to the community; Government needs to do more.*

Downs, A. (1972). Up and down with ecology—The 'issue-attention cycle.' *The Public Interest, 28,* 38-50.

Goffman, E. (1961). *Asylums.* Garden City, NY: Anchor Books.

Goldman, H., Gattozzi, A., & Taube, C. (1981). Defining and counting the chronically mentally ill. *Hospital and Community Psychiatry, 32*(1), 21-27.

Gusfield, J. (1963). *Symbolic crusade.* Urbana, IL: University of Illinois Press.

Gusfield, J. (1981). *The culture of public problems.* Chicago: University of Chicago Press.

Harding, C. (1985). Paper presented at CSWE conference, "The Chronically Mentally Ill: Improving the Knowledge Base through Research," 13-14 June 1985, Washington, D.C.

Harrington, M. (1962). *The other America.* Baltimore: Penguin Books.

HEW Task Force (1978). *Report of the HEW task force on implementation of the report to the president from the President's Commission on Mental Health.*

Hogarty, G. et al. (1973). Drug and sociotherapy in the aftercare of schizophrenic patients, *Archives of General Psychiatry, 28,* 54-64.

Joint Commission on Mental Illness and Health (1961). *Action for mental health.* New York: John Wiley & Sons.

Kirk, S.A. (1976). Effectiveness of community services for discharged mental hospital patients. *American Journal of Orthopsychiatry, 46*(4), 646-659.

Kirk, S. & Therrien, M. (1975). Community mental health myths and the fate of former hospitalized patients. *Psychiatry, 38,* 209-217.

Nuehring, E. & Markle, G. (1974). Nicotine and norms: The re-emergence of a deviant behavior. *Social problems, 21*(4), 513-526.

President's Commission on Mental Health (1978). *Report to the President.* Washington, D.C.: U.S. Printing Office.

Scheff, T. (1966). *Being mentally ill: A sociological theory.* Chicago: Aldine.

Segal, S. & Baumohl, J. (1982). The new chronic patient: The creation of an underserved population, in L. Snowden (Ed.), *Reaching the underserved.* Beverly Hills: Sage, 95-116.

Stern, Mark M. (1984). The emergence of the homeless as a public problem. *Social Service Review, 58*(2), 291-301.

U.S. Department of Health and Human Services (1980). *National plan for the chronically mentally ill.*